BUYING
REAL ESTATE
OVERSEAS
FOR
CASH FLOW
(AND A BETTER LIFE)

Get Started with as Little as $50,000

BUYING
REAL ESTATE
OVERSEAS
FOR
CASH FLOW
(AND A BETTER LIFE)

KATHLEEN PEDDICORD AND **LIEF SIMON**

WILEY

Published by John Wiley & Sons, Inc., Hoboken, New Jersey.
Published simultaneously in Canada.

For general information on our other products and services or for technical support, please contact our Customer Care Department within the United States at (800) 762-2974, outside the United States at (317) 572-3993 or fax (317) 572-4002.

Wiley publishes in a variety of print and electronic formats and by print-on-demand. Some material included with standard print versions of this book may not be included in e-books or in print-on-demand. If this book refers to media such as a CD or DVD that is not included in the version you purchased, you may download this material at http://booksupport.wiley.com. For more information about Wiley products, visit www.wiley.com.

Limited portions of this book were previously published in *How to Buy Real Estate Overseas* (ISBN 9781118518595) by Kathleen Peddicord.

Library of Congress Cataloging-in-Publication Data

Names: Peddicord, Kathleen, author. | Simon, Lief, author.
Title: Buying real estate overseas for cash flow (and a better life) : get
   started with as little as $50,000 / Kathleen Peddicord, Lief Simon.
Description: First Edition. | Hoboken : Wiley, 2020. | Includes index.
Identifiers: LCCN 2020010575 (print) | LCCN 2020010576 (ebook) | ISBN
   9781119696209 (paperback) | ISBN 9781119696254 (adobe pdf) | ISBN
   9781119696230 (epub)
Subjects: LCSH: Real estate investment—Foreign countries. | Retirement,
   Places of—Foreign countries. | Retirees—Life skills guides. |
   Americans—Foreign countries.
Classification: LCC HD1382.5 .P434 2020 (print) | LCC HD1382.5 (ebook) |
   DDC 332.63/24—dc23
LC record available at https://lccn.loc.gov/2020010575
LC ebook record available at https://lccn.loc.gov/2020010576

COVER DESIGN: PAUL MCCARTHY
COVER ART: © GETTY IMAGES | BY EVE LIVESEY

Printed in the United States of America

SKY10041922_012523

For Kaitlin and Jackson

Contents

Preface

Strategic Advice and Recommendations
Amidst and Post the Coronavirus Pandemic—Challenges
and Opportunities for Cash Flow Investors Overseas

As this book goes to press, more than 90% of the U.S. population and more than 20% of the entire global population are under instructions to stay at home and shelter in place. Millions of workers are filing for first-time unemployment, and trillions of dollars have been erased from stock portfolios. We humans are living through the greatest health crisis since the Spanish flu of 1918 and could face the biggest market meltdown since the Great Depression. The personal and financial challenges we're navigating are existential, the pain and hardship they're creating overwhelming.

What do they mean in the context of these pages?

We believe the COVID-19 crisis is also going to lead to one of the greatest buyer's markets the world has ever seen. Overleveraged owners, bankrupt businesses, desperate sellers, and rock-bottom currency values will translate to the fire-sale of a generation if not the century. The eighteenth-century British nobleman and banker Baron Rothschild said it so we don't have to. You should buy when there's blood in the streets, and that's the view today.

With the help of contacts in key markets worldwide, we're taking stock of pre-crisis trends, property listings, government interventions, currency values, and COVID-19 casualties. We want to be prepared to act as soon as it makes sense to do so, and we recommend you do the same.

Because, eventually, the pandemic will be contained and global markets and economies will recover, and, again, the fallout from the crisis will present the world with unprecedented investment opportunity. Perhaps more important, however, the experience of having lived through this period will leave us with a reinforced and maybe a reinvented understanding of what matters most in life.

Considered from a post-crisis perspective, where in the world will offer the best options for diversifying your investment portfolio and, at the same time, your lifestyle? Where should you look now to embrace the many opportunities our world continues to offer while positioning yourself for cash flow, upside, and security in the face of whatever tomorrow brings? We think we must consider that COVID-19 is not the only global catastrophe we could face in our lifetimes. Given that position, we further believe it is more critical than it has ever been to expand where you spend your time and your money so you're not at the mercy of any single government, economy, marketplace, or currency.

We have a moment now, while the world sits on collective pause, to regroup on what we'd like our lives to look like and to connect the dots between our ideal lifestyle and the top choices for the best places to think about spending time while making money overseas.

Our overriding objective in these pages is to show you how to build a diversified portfolio of hard assets overseas to generate cash flow to fund the lifestyle, the retirement, and the legacy you want. So, as we consider our world post-pandemic, let's start there.

What will global property markets look like post the COVID-19 crisis?

We do not believe we're going to see 40–70% drops as we did in the wake of the 2008/2009 global crisis, when real estate markets worldwide took huge hits with few exceptions. However, localized markets and individual properties will experience those levels of price reductions, even if only in U.S. dollar terms.

The Crisis Will Create a Supercharged U.S. Dollar

That is to say, one of the biggest opportunities created by the current crisis is going to have to do with supercharged U.S. dollar buying power. The Colombian peso and Brazilian real, for example, have weakened significantly against the U.S. dollar since the virus crisis began. These countries are oil exporters and commodity producers. The values of their currencies depend on their abilities to sell those products on the global market in dollars and then trade those dollars back into pesos and reals. Will the Colombian peso or the real return to pre-virus levels once the crisis abates and oil prices begin to recover? Probably. Meanwhile, properties in these countries will stand out as crisis-level buys for U.S. dollar holders.

How Long Until Tourist Rental Markets Recover?

Short-term rentals are a key element of any global property portfolio, a top choice for generating diversified cash flow overseas. What's the post-COVID-19 picture for this asset class?

The vacation rental business disappeared overnight when borders closed and planes stopped flying. Hotels are being converted to hospitals in some countries, and short-term rentals are being relisted as long term. That's one benefit of owning a furnished rental. You can reposition it according to market demand. In Dublin, Ireland, for example, the available inventory of long-term rentals jumped 83% in March 2020 compared with March 2019, while short-term rental listings on Airbnb fell accordingly.

Since the advent of Airbnb, many cities have seen sharp declines in long-term rental supply, increasing the cost of housing for locals. In an active tourist destination, a short-term rental can produce a much higher net yield than one rented long term. Now we're going to see a dramatic shift, which is good news for locals looking for affordable housing but not necessarily for global property investors. However, we believe this is a temporary trend and will revert as tourist markets are reborn.

You can easily switch a rental from short to long term in a European city, but making a change like that won't get you far in a resort town like Playa del Carmen, Mexico, where's there's next to zero long-term rental demand. Expect, therefore, to see hugely discounted vacation rental prices in destinations like Playa del Carmen when people begin traveling again. Also expect to see properties for sale at discounted prices from owners who either need to sell their investment real estate to shore up their personal financial situations back home or because an extended loss of cash flow has put them behind on their mortgage payments. As we remind our Live and Invest Overseas readers often, leverage is a double-edged sword.

Look for More Seller Financing Options

Speaking of leverage, note that banks in countries where financing has been an option for foreign buyers will be focused on helping locals recover first. We think, therefore, that institutional financing options for us foreign investors will become thinner on the ground for a period.

On the other hand, we also predict that global property buyers will find sellers and developers more open to more creative terms than they've been in a long time, especially in Latin American markets dependent on foreign buyers. Seller financing will be particularly easier to come by in Panama and Belize, for example.

Buy on These Dips

Some markets in Europe are already experiencing broad real estate price drops. Greece is top of this list. We believe this country will represent a bona-fide blood-in-the-streets opportunity, and we will share specific opportunities with our Live and Invest Overseas readers in real time. (You can stay up to date with these opportunities as a reader of our free e-letter service. Go to www .liveandinvestoverseas.com/cashflowupdates to sign up.)

In addition, we expect prices in Portugal, where values had appreciated significantly between 2015 and 2019—particularly in Lisbon, Porto, and Lagos—to soften and perhaps to fall when pent-up supply is released after Europe reopens. The window of opportunity here, though, will be short.

We predict price drops across Latin America. Emerging markets are going to be hardest hit by the pandemic crisis, and their economies will be slowest to recover. This means countries at the top of your post-crisis opportunity list should include Mexico, Belize, and Brazil.

Panama is an exception in this regard in this part of the world. This country reacted quickly to the coronavirus threat, showing itself again to be more than just another banana republic. Panama closed its borders in a matter of days, then restricted the movement of its residents in inventive ways. At the height of the threat, women were allowed to leave their homes at assigned two-hour increments on Mondays, Wednesdays, and Fridays, while men were able to be out for two hours at a time only on Tuesdays, Thursdays, and Saturdays. Everyone had to stay home Sundays, and the government banned the sale of alcohol. No baby boom for Panama but we predict a quicker return of economic activity certainly than anywhere else in the region. In addition, our contacts in the country report that President Laurentino "Nito" Cortizo's administration is planning an aggressive program of investor incentives to attract direct foreign investment post-pandemic lockdown. Again, we'll keep our Live and Invest Overseas readers up to date on these programs as they are rolled out, at www.liveandinvestoverseas.com/cashflowupdates.

The Winningest of All Cash-Flow Investments Overseas

The second cash-flowing asset class every diversified global property portfolio should include is agriculture. Amidst and in the wake of the COVID-19 crisis, this investment option remains the big winner. While short-term rentals are producing zero cash flow during the global shutdown, agricultural properties are still growing food … and people are still eating.

Meaning crops need to be harvested. The United States, Germany, and other developed-world markets rely on migrant workers for their harvests. With borders closed, farmers in these countries are worried about how they're going to bring in their crops before they rot in the fields. In the countries we recommend in these pages for turnkey agriculture investment—Panama and Thailand are at the top of this list—farmers don't rely on migrant labor. They use seasonal workers, but recruit them locally. One more benefit of diversification.

The most resilient part of any real estate investment portfolio during the current or any other crisis will be timber. Trees don't care about a virus. And, even with less attention from caretakers, they keep growing.

Three Countries We like Best Post-Pandemic

Our objective in the pages that follow is to show you how to generate the cash flow you need to be able to afford the lifestyle you want. Looking ahead to the other side of today's crisis, what might you want your life to look like and where in the world might you be able to realize that ideal? Here are three places where you could restart your life putting health, self-resilience, and community first, while also investing in diversified, income-producing hard assets:

#1: Portugal's Algarve Coast

At home on Portugal's coast, you could wake every morning to the sound of local fisherman announcing the morning's catch and the soft chimes of bicycle bells signaling the start of the daily commute. Offshore this 100-mile-long stretch, the Atlantic Ocean crashes, as it has for centuries, carving arches, coves, and caves into the sandstone, creating a picture-postcard view at every turn. Portugal's Algarve region is not only a top option for retirement in Europe but one of the best places in the world to live, thanks to its

Year-Round Sunshine

Portugal enjoys one of the most stable climates in the world and 3,300 hours of sunshine per year, meaning more sunny days than almost anywhere else in Europe. The Algarve coast has no bad weather months.

Safety

Portugal ranks as the third-safest country in the world. Violent crime is rare, and petty crime is limited to pickpocketing during the busy tourist season. As well, this country has managed to keep itself separate from the immigration crisis that is playing out in other parts of Europe.

Good Infrastructure

Portugal has enjoyed important infrastructure investments in recent years, specifically to do with the country's highway network and airports. As a result, this is a great base for exploring all Europe and North Africa.

International Standard Health Care

Health care in Portugal is high quality and a fraction the cost of health care in the United States. If you become a resident, public health care is free.

Golf

Portugal's Algarve region boasts 42 courses in less than 100 miles.

Great Beaches

The European Blue Flag Association has awarded 88 beaches along the Algarve coast Blue Flag status, recognizing their excellent water quality and environmental standards.

Affordable Cost of Living

The cost of living in Portugal is among the lowest in Western Europe, on average 30% lower than in any other country in the region. A couple could live here modestly but comfortably on a budget of as little as 1,300 euros per month. With a budget of 2,000 euros per month or more, you could enjoy a fully appointed lifestyle in this heart of the Old World. And right now your dollars buy a lot of euros.

The Language

English is widely spoken. Living here, you could get by without learning to speak Portuguese.

Healthy Living

The Portuguese are the biggest fish eaters per capital in Europe, and fresh fish of great variety is available in the ever-present daily markets. The year-round sunshine and fertile earth in this part of the world mean an abundance of fresh produce, too, also available in the local markets. Meantime, pollution rates are low, and streets, towns, and beaches are clean and litter-free.

Retiree Residency

Portugal offers the most user-friendly residency option in the eurozone. You can qualify to live in the country full time simply by showing a reliable income of at least 1,200 euros per month.

#2: Mazatlan, Mexico

For decades, Americans have voted Mexico the world's best place to live or retire in the way that really counts—they've packed up and moved there. This country is home to between 1 and 2 million American expats and retirees, more than any other country. Its biggest advantage is its accessibility. Living or retired on Mexico's Pacific coast, you can come and go from the United States by car. Moving to Mexico can be as hassle-free as an international move gets. Nothing's as easy as loading up a truck and driving south. Your entire moving budget could be gas and tolls.

Why else does Mazatlán stand out as a top Plan B option?

Familiarity

From its administrative set-up (the Mexican government is a stable democracy, with executive, legislative, and judicial branches functioning in a similar way to those in the United States) to its big-footprint shopping, Mexico is familiar and therefore comfortable. If you're itching for an adventure in a foreign land that's not too foreign, Mexico could be the experience you seek.

Language

All the North American attention from both expats and tourists means that many Mexicans, especially in the service industry, speak English. This can make things like navigating the residency process at the immigration office and managing the real estate purchase process with your attorney much easier.

Property Markets

Property markets in many areas of Mexico are soft and growing softer thanks to current global events. In addition, the U.S. dollar is at an historic high against the Mexican peso, meaning you having supercharged buying power in those Mexican markets where real estate trades in pesos.

Easy Residency

Automatic six-month tourist stays and easy and fast immigration make it possible to come and go and spend as much time in the country as you'd like. You can maintain a second home here (a place you rent out when you're not using it yourself, say) without having to bother with the expense of obtaining formal resident status.

Keep Your Medicare

Living in Mazatlán, you could return easily to the United States to use Medicare. If you're considering this move as a retiree, nearing or over the age of 65, this can be Mexico's most compelling advantage. Mexico offers excellent health care, but Medicare won't pay for it—with limited exceptions, Medicare doesn't cross any border. However, if you retire in Mexico, you'd be only a drive or quick flight away from accessing your benefits.

This means keeping and continuing to pay for Medicare coverage in addition to any other health insurance you might opt for. This can be a good strategy for a Medicare-eligible retiree moving to any foreign country, a safety net.

The Cost of Living

While the living is not as cheap as it was in the 1970s when Americans began migrating to Mexico in volume, it's a global bargain and more of a budgeter's delight right now than it's been in a long time, thanks to the U.S. dollar's strength.

In some parts of the country, this translates to super real estate deals. But even where real estate trades in U.S. dollars, the strong dollar makes everything else—from a liter of gasoline and a week's worth of groceries to a suite of bedroom furniture and a night out on the town—a bargain. Two can dine five star, enjoying three courses and good wine, for less than 50 bucks.

#3: Cayo, Belize

Belize remains off the world's radar. Nobody is targeting or intent on stirring up trouble in this little country that's part Caribbean, part Central American. Most people don't give Belize a second thought. In today's world, that's a plus.

The country is one of the most important members of the Caribbean Community, thanks to its arable land and agricultural capacity. It helps provide food security for CARICOM, an international community of primarily small English-speaking island nations.

Belize has pristine marine, rainforest, and riverine environments and a small population, so, in addition to being food secure, it is a great vacation destination and an ideal place to live. Cayo is the breadbasket of Belize principally because of the industriousness of the Mennonites of Spanish Lookout, a booming town with thriving businesses and a back-to-basics, traditional way of life.

The U.S. Department of Agriculture estimates that the average American meal travels 1,500 miles from farm to market. The movement is toward sourcing food from within 100 miles. In Cayo, your food could be sourced within 10 miles. Living here, you could even enjoy a zero-mile diet. Imported foods are available if you want them, but it's possible in Cayo to be food secure and not dependent upon an elaborate, vulnerable, and costly global supply chain.

Here are six more reasons Cayo, Belize, is an ideal option for a self-sufficient, resilient, sustainable, neighborly, and fun life …

Reliable Water Sources

Residents of Cayo catch, store, and filter rainwater, and groundwater is likewise in abundant supply. The rivers this area is known for provide a sometime alternative for garden irrigation and an everyday option for fishing.

Energy Independence

Living off-grid with solar and rain-catchment doesn't have to mean giving up the amenities of the modern world. In Cayo, you can live a fully self-sufficient life that includes high-speed internet, modern appliances, and all other comforts of the twenty-first century.

Low Population Density

During a disruption in the supply chain, as we are seeing now, it's good to be a safe distance from big, dense cities. Belize has a population density of just 37 people per square mile. The whole country feels like a small town. The small population makes it easy to become part of the community, and both locals and expats who've settled here are welcoming and willing to lend a hand or make an effort for a neighbor.

English Speaking

As a former English colony (and still a part of the English Commonwealth), Belize is the only officially English-speaking country in Central America. One of the biggest challenges you can face when making a move to a new country is communicating with your new neighbors. Anywhere you might think about moving, including Belize, you'll have to learn to overcome and adapt to cultural differences. A language difference makes that and everything else – from giving directions to a taxi driver and filling a prescription at the pharmacy to getting your broken hot water heater fixed and negotiating for the purchase of a new home – more difficult. In Belize, you don't have to worry about learning a new language if you don't want to.

Great Weather

The country is blessed with abundant year-round sunshine. The rainy season extends from June to November but, even during those months, skies are sunny more than they're not. The reliable sunshine makes for happy, healthy living and also a great growing environment.

Little Crime

Some small areas of Belize City suffer from a drug trade, gangs, and the activities that come with those cultures. However, those are localized neighborhoods. Avoid them. Otherwise, Belize is one of the safest places on earth and far removed from twenty-first-century troubles.

The Surest Strategy in the Race to Wealth, Health, Freedom, and Security

The surest way to prepare for whatever tomorrow brings is to diversify beyond your home borders, both your life and your investments. If you're searching for options right now, wondering what to do in the face of the current global landscape, we urge you to remember this critical truth. It's crisis times like these when a diversified lifestyle and a truly globally diversified portfolio of hard assets really pay off. So set the worrying aside. It only drains your energy and slows your progress.

How can you make sure you come through this crisis stage not only whole but stronger than ever? You must diversify into hard assets to generate cash flow overseas. It is the smartest strategy for protecting and growing wealth, especially in times of crisis. Gold prices and stock markets continue on a roller coaster. Real estate remains the slow and steady tortoise in the race to wealth and security.

Introduction

Earning Cash Flow from Real Estate Overseas Is the Same as Earning Cash Flow from Real Estate at Home … with These Three Important Differences

"It's perfect. I'll take it. How much is it?"

So said the Irish hairdresser to the Montenegrin real estate agent.

The agent was touring the young woman through an apartment for sale in the medieval town of Kotor. The woman didn't get past the entryway before making her buy decision. Indeed, she had been ready to invest before boarding the plane from Dublin. She was desperate to take her first step onto the property ladder but didn't qualify for financing at home in Ireland (the "do you have a pulse?" mortgages didn't become common in this country until a year later). No bother. Everyone was buying property abroad. She would, too.

The agent who sold the hairdresser that Kotor apartment told me the story when Lief met him the following week. We, too, were considering an investment in Montenegro.

It was 2004 and that agent (like all real estate agents in the country) was selling properties faster than he could count the commissions. All Europe and a few Americans like us were competing with each other to get into the hottest new property market on the Continent. Unlike the hairdresser, we didn't invest. The math didn't work.

That young woman from Dublin, like too many novice and even many experienced investors, was buying because she was certain the value of what she was buying was going to increase. She didn't bother to ask about the potential for rental yield or try to project the cash flow she could expect.

She (we assume and would have loved to have had a way to confirm), along with multitudes of other global property investors, learned the hard way and only four years later that, when investing in real estate, rising prices are not guaranteed. The 2008 crash wiped out values worldwide and, with them, investors who hadn't run the numbers but had bought for appreciation rather than yield.

Property values move up and down and matter only if you're selling the property. Cash flow can be reliable and is always bankable. Buying for appreciation is chasing paper profits. Buying for cash flow is putting money in your pocket.

What Frank Lloyd Wright Taught Us About Other People's Money

Lief's first real estate purchase was in Chicago. He was renting in a three-flat when the owner sent a notice to all the tenants informing them he was listing the property for sale. It was a Frank Lloyd Wright building. Lief's apartment was big, the layout comfortable. He didn't want to give it up, so, rather than considering where he might move, Lief began figuring out a way to buy the building where he was living. Unfortunately, the people living on the top floor had the same idea and approached the owner with a plan to convert the building into condos so they could buy their apartment. That inflated the price in the seller's mind.

Undaunted, Lief put together a spreadsheet to see if he could make the numbers work for an outright purchase. He'd continue living in his apartment, paying himself rent, and rent out the other two. He calculated that he could charge more for those other units, as the current rents were below market.

Banks were offering special programs for first-time buyers. Lief knew he could get a loan. The question was whether the cash-flow math worked. Would the three apartments generate enough income to support the mortgage?

Using leverage to buy a rental property is a common strategy in the United States. The theory is that the rent pays back the bank, month by month, and covers your other expenses, hopefully with some cash flow left over. Meanwhile, equity builds up as the mortgage gets paid down ... while, in theory, the property's value appreciates. How to buy with other people's money (OPM) is the first strategy you learn at any real estate investment seminar.

Lief obtained a mortgage with a loan-to-value ratio (LTV) of 98%. However, it wasn't for the building where he was living. His neighbor's condo plan botched that deal. But the seed had been planted and the spreadsheet created. Lief's math showed him what to do next.

He found a real estate agent and explained his parameters. Today we make buy decisions based on projected rental yields, gross and net. For this first purchase Lief didn't think beyond paying the mortgage.

He spent four months considering dozens of properties and entering the details for each into his spreadsheet. Two-flat buildings never came close to break-even cash flow, though Lief figures he probably could have made the math work for many of the buildings he looked at by increasing his own rent, but he didn't want to do that. Again, his stubbornness paid off (as he likes to point out for Kathleen's benefit). Lief kept active in the market, looking daily at new listings, until he found a property that fit his requirements. It was a building that had come back onto the market after the woman who had signed a purchase contract for it failed to qualify for financing. She was a hairdresser (but not Irish).

The price was good. The location was within the zone Lief had targeted. Most important, the numbers worked. Lief could keep paying himself the same rent and would be able to cover the mortgage even without increasing the rent for the other two apartments.

We met two-and-a-half years later, when, coincidentally, we both were making plans to move to Ireland. We were engaged two-and-a-half months after we met and married two months after that. Then we moved together—Lief from Chicago, Kathleen from Baltimore—to Waterford. The timing was ideal for selling Lief's three-flat. The Chicago market was frothy. He set the price above the going market rate, and the building still sold quickly. He walked away with 80% more than he'd paid less than three years earlier. The leveraged return on Lief's 2% down payment was 3,000%. He had turned $5,000 into $150,000 *after* closing costs and commissions. And he'd had positive cash flow from rental income every month he had owned the building.

It was an as-good-as-it-gets property investment experience, first because Lief made the buy decision based on cash flow math and second because he was able to leverage the purchase.

Buying with OPM can—as any property investor will tell you—mean an upside, but it comes with risk. It doesn't matter what your property is worth if the cash flow it generates doesn't cover the mortgage. We've known too many U.S. real estate investors who have lost too many properties when market changes collapsed their highly leveraged portfolios.

Even though we've benefited from it, we don't preach the OPM mantra. Twenty-five years of experience across 24 markets worldwide, including the United States, have taught us to respect the fundamentals. We don't buy unless the projected net rental yields translate into cash flow enough to support the investment.

Never Invest for 2% Thinking Appreciation Will Make Up the Difference

After Lief sold that three-flat in Chicago and we made our move to Ireland, we began analyzing Irish real estate markets looking for investment opportunities. At the time (1999), most rental properties in this country were generating net yields of 2% or less. Dismal. But the Irish didn't care. Property values across the country had been appreciating 10% a year or more for years, and the Irish expected that to continue indefinitely.

They were investing and reinvesting using OPM. Banks were lending easily (though not yet at 2005 levels, when 110% LTV mortgages—the extra 10% to cover the "stamp duty" required at closing—were being handed out like chocolate buttons to tykes at Christmas). Investors were subsidizing mortgage payments out of pocket because rents weren't doing the job. They saw it as a sensible ongoing investment in the windfall appreciation they were certain would come.

In 2008, Irish property values fell 50% and more, depending on the region of the country, almost overnight. Most of those 110% LTV-financed properties were returned to the bank. Didn't seem so clever any longer to top-up mortgage payments out of pocket.

Leverage isn't always a good idea and, when investing overseas, it isn't always—or at least not always easily—available. In Part II, we'll detail your realistic financing options, but you should understand as you set out to start and then grow your global cash flow portfolio that OPM isn't always an option. Sometimes that's for the best.

Ignore Gross Returns Because It's Only the Net That Matters

The math is the same whether you're calculating the rental yield for a property in Arizona or Argentina. The expenses, though, can be different, and this is the second critical factor to take into account when projecting cash flow from a property investment overseas. Calculate what your return will be gross and then ignore that figure. Only the net matters.

In Ecuador, for example, the tenant pays the homeowner's association (HOA) fee on top of the rent. Some countries impose a withholding tax on gross rental income when it's paid; you recover any overpayment by filing an annual tax return. And management fees for short-term rentals can range from 15% to 35% and more, depending on the market.

A gross rental yield of 25% sounds great until you calculate the expenses and find that it nets to 3% after backing out management splits, building fees, and other higher-than-typical expenses for that particular property. Looking only at the top-line return, you could dismiss a gross rental yield of 12% that nets to 6% in the same market.

Nondollar Cash Flow Can Fund Local Adventures

The third difference between buying real estate for cash flow in the United States and buying real estate for cash flow overseas is that often the cash flows in a different currency. Like OPM, this is a potential upside and also a potential risk.

In 2015, we went shopping for a rental apartment on Portugal's Algarve coast. After eight years of economic crisis, this country was at a bottom and we perceived turning the corner. After exploring several beach towns and villages, we focused on Lagos, where we toured six properties and liked one in particular for its location, undervalued price, and motivated seller. Our math, based on data from the real estate agent and our own market research, projected a net annual return of 8%. Our general net yield expectation from a rental anywhere is 5% to 8%. We made an offer and proceeded with the purchase.

Other apartments we looked at in Lagos projected as good or better net rental yields and came with similarly appealing price tags. We chose the apartment we did because we agreed we would be happy owning it even if it didn't rent well or at all. When you're buying, rental projections are just that. You don't know what your yield will be until you begin earning it.

The apartment we bought was in the center of the town, on a winding, cobblestoned, pedestrian-only street, with easy access to shops and restaurants, and it had a rooftop terrace with an ocean view. We could use the place for personal vacations, we told ourselves as we stood on the roof looking out at the sea, in addition to or even instead of renting it out. And we did. During the four years we owned the property, we visited four times. During those stays, we withdrew some of the euro cash accumulated from apartment rent paid into our Portugal bank account and used that money to cover our expenses. It was like a series of free holidays in a fifteenth-century town on Europe's sunny southern coast. In addition to vacation mad money, the rental cash flow covered all expenses associated with the apartment and left us with a nice-sized and steadily growing euro nest egg.

The rental return met our 8% projection the first year and hit our 5% to 8% mark each of the four years we owned it, based on the original purchase price. The problem, if you want to call it that, was that markets across Portugal, including in Lagos, appreciated quickly after this country turned its crisis corner. During a visit to Lagos four years after our purchase, a friend in the local real estate industry suggested we think about selling our apartment.

"I'm certain you could get more than twice what you paid," he told us.

We didn't believe him, but two other local agents concurred. Calculated on the much higher valuation, our net rental return was less than 3%. At that yield, we're sellers rather than buyers.

All real estate in the Algarve appreciated over the four years we owned our Lagos apartment, but our apartment more than doubled in value. Part of the reason was the location and the type of property. It worked as a rental, but it was also comfortable for full-time living. In addition, the place had a charm factor that set it apart. It wasn't one of the cookie-cutter beach-resort condos you find along this coast. That *je ne sais quoi* element was part of the reason we bought in the first place. It's not a data point you can enter into your spreadsheet when shopping, but it is something to remember when comparing properties for potential purchase. Building a portfolio of cash-flowing properties overseas is a chance to make money and build wealth, yes, but it's also a chance to improve your lifestyle. Remember that—sometimes even prioritize that—when making investment choices.

The exchange rate between the euro and the U.S. dollar didn't move much over the four years we owned the property in Portugal, but it could have. This is another reason it's better to buy in places where you want not only to make money but also to spend time. We were happy to spend the euros we were earning locally, meaning we were insulated against potential currency downside. It didn't matter to us if the euro lost ground on the dollar, because we weren't converting our euros into dollars. We were spending and accumulating them in euroland.

Likewise, when we sold that apartment, we kept the proceeds in euros, ready for a next EU investment.

The Currency Factor

That said, when investing in real estate that trades hands in something other than your base currency, you need to be prepared for the potential consequences. If timing is on your side, a fluctuating currency exchange rate can boost your total home currency return. If not, it can erode it.

We have had both experiences over the 25 years we've been investing in real estate overseas. We invested once in a hard money loan with (that is, we lent money to) a developer in Australia who was offering an annualized return of 12% for an 18-month term. When we made the investment, the U.S. dollar was strong against the Aussie dollar. Over the course of the 18 months that we held the investment, the U.S. dollar weakened. As a result, after the loan had been repaid, our total return in U.S. dollar terms was 12% plus an additional 30%, thanks to the currency movement. Nice surprise upside, right?

On the other hand, when we invested in Medellín, Colombia, in 2011, the Colombian peso was at an historic high against the U.S. dollar. Today, the situation is reversed. While our apartment in that city is worth more than three times what we paid for it in peso terms, it's worth about twice as much in dollar terms. That matters, though, only if we sell and convert the resulting pesos into dollars. We have no need to sell and so continue watching the property's value appreciate while waiting for the peso to rebound.

Market values move up and down. Currency exchange rates fluctuate in cycles. Cash flow carries you through, meaning that cash-flow math is the key to success.

However, This Is Not Only About the Money

When investing for cash flow overseas, you want to make buy decisions based on the cash-flow math, but you also want to remember the big picture. This is an investment strategy, yes, but, more important, it's a lifestyle. So, before you begin considering where or what to buy, ask yourself what you want your life to look like. That's the place to start. What life objectives are you hoping to achieve? For the best outcome, you want to marry those with your investment goals.

Fundamentally, the real advantage of this strategy is diversification of your portfolio and assets but also of your life, your retirement, and your legacy.

We are living at a time that presents the opportunity to take the investor's profit agenda, combine it with the live-better-for-less agenda of the retiree, and transfer it overseas. You have a chance right now to use overseas real estate as both an investment vehicle and a program for a new and better life, both immediately and longer term in retirement. Overseas real estate amounts to the surest strategy for creating and preserving legacy wealth while simultaneously reinventing your life and rescuing your retirement. Many options exist for where to buy to make money while also making a new life, and, thanks to our Age of the Internet, it is possible today to seize these opportunities easily and cost-effectively to build a new life while staying in real-time touch with family, friends, business concerns, and investment portfolios from the old one.

The best case is when you are able to find a piece of real estate in a place where you want to spend time, short term on vacation and long term in retirement, that also holds out the potential for cash flow and an investment return. This perfect storm of objectives should be your ultimate goal. A holiday home on the coast of Panama can become little more than a headache and a carrying cost if you ultimately decide you can't abide life in the tropics.

Could You Really Do This?

The reasons to diversify your investment portfolio and your lifestyle to include cash-flowing real estate overseas have never been more compelling than they are right now. But, you may be thinking, who does this, really? Isn't this a strategy of the jet set? No, it's not.

Lief comes from middle-class Phoenix, Kathleen from middle-class Baltimore. We started our overseas real estate adventures with next-to-nothing. Lief made that first property investment we told you about in Chicago using a $5,000 gift from a family member. Over the decades that we've been living this life, we've met countless others who also have built adventure-filled lives that include cash-flow-generating real estate holdings overseas, and we can't think of one of them we'd describe as jet set. These are all regular folks.

The idea of diversifying your investments, your assets, your life, and your future overseas can seem intimidating, even paralyzing. Could you really do it? Based on more than 25 years of experience, we can tell you confidently that the answer to that question is yes.

The two most common reasons for resisting the idea of investing in real estate overseas can be a general uncertainty about how to go about it and a more specific concern about the cost. Can the average investor or retiree really afford to pursue this strategy? Again, yes. You could get started with as little as $50,000 to $100,000 of working capital, sometimes less.

How can you be sure something won't go wrong? You can't. There are risks, and, as with any kind of investing, nothing is guaranteed. Don't let that deter you. What's the option? To do nothing? To keep your assets, your retirement, and your future all at home, all in one place? Would that be safer or more prudent? No.

You must diversify, both your investments and your life. It's a necessity of the world we're living in. Here's your chance to do that while creating healthy and steady cash flow to fund an adventure-filled lifestyle in retirement or starting right now.

We're here to walk you through it.

Buying Real Estate Overseas Is Not Only a Top Cash-flow Strategy—It's Also a Sure Way to Improve Your Lifestyle

That Belize condo or Paris apartment rental earning you 8% net per year could also be your second home in the Caribbean or your Old World retirement plan. Investing in real estate overseas is not only about the money. It's also the surest way we know to inject strong doses of romance and adventure into your life ... while perhaps significantly reducing your cost of living. Owning property in a foreign country can seem like a jet-set strategy because it can be a jet-set strategy. The thing is you don't need anything like a jet-setter's budget to pursue it.

1

Buy Overseas to Make Travel and Adventure Part of Your Life Right Now

But haven't we done this already? Haven't we already bought an old stone house surrounded by mud? Isn't that what we did in Ireland? Why do you guys want to do this again?

In 2004, Lief, our two children, and I spent a week touring around Istria, Croatia, with a focused agenda. We were in the market for one of the old white stone houses you find across this peninsula. To that end, we drove Kaitlin, 15, and Jackson, 5, in one car, and our property agent followed along behind in hers, from one stone farmhouse to another, up and down the narrow winding roads of these mountainsides, through the medieval villages, and past the ever-present fields of olive trees, grape vines, and sunflowers.

We had recently made our move from Ireland to France and, one rainy morning of that Istrian family adventure, standing in one more muddy Istrian farmyard, Kaitlin shared her observation. Probably she wasn't the only one wondering what we were doing. Having just relocated to Paris, where we were still in the process of renovating the apartment that would be our home in that city, busy with business and investment projects, why had we gotten it into our heads that we wanted to buy a 200-year-old house on the side of a mountain in the middle of the Istrian peninsula?

Because we liked it there. We wanted to stake our small claim to this beautiful and historic region that, during previous visits in previous years, had captured our hearts and our imaginations. We believed in the future of Croatia, a country with an extraordinarily complicated past and an extremely open-minded, forward-looking population. We recognized, at the time, that Croatia was at another turning point in its long history, and we wanted to be part of it.

Plus, the Istrian peninsula, we'd observed for some time, serves up some of the most delightful scenery on this planet. The land seems to rise up to embrace you. Everywhere you look, something nice is growing—olives, grapes, figs, tomatoes, pumpkins, blackberries, wildflowers. Even the buildings seem to be of the earth, built of its white stone and red clay. In some parts of the world, Nature outdoes herself. In others, that which man has built is impressive. In Istria, Nature and mankind have worked together over centuries, starting with the Romans, to create a land of delights you have to see to appreciate.

So that rainy morning in that muddy farmyard, with Kaitlin and probably others, too, questioning our sense, we decided that we'd found the old white stone house we'd come looking for, made an offer to the Istrian owner, and agreed on the terms with a handshake. The seller sealed the deal by making a gift to us of lavender oil his wife had bottled.

Before you're ready to retire, you're likely to notice places around the world where you'd like to be able to spend time. Not just once every several years or so in a hotel, but more regularly, as often as possible, in the company of your family and friends, and in a place of your own. That's the realization we made years ago in Istria, Croatia.

When you identify a destination that meets this description, we recommend you take stock of the bigger picture, considering, first, whether that destination is also a place where you think you might like to spend time long term, either full or part time, and second, if the real estate market there presents potential for cash flow. If the answer to either of those questions is yes (and certainly if the answer to both of those questions is yes), then you've found your ideal second home overseas.

In our case, with Istria, the answer to both taking-stock questions was enthusiastically positive, and, so, we pushed ahead. Whereas the house in Waterford and the apartment in Paris, for example, were purchased because we needed places to live at the time, we bought the property in Istria because we decided that this region was a part of the world we wanted an excuse to return to as often as we could manage.

The ideal property purchase overseas can be a holiday home that also qualifies as an investment and that could play a role in your retirement plan. This was what tipped the scales for us with the purchase in Istria. The old farmhouse came with a bit of land. On that land, we daydreamed, we could cultivate olives, figs, even grapes. Maybe we could try making our own wine! We could go for long hikes in the hills, exploring the medieval villages nearby, by day, then read by firelight come evening.

We returned to these ideas again and again and finally rationalized them with the agreement that this was a market we believed in. Croatians, we noted, were tired of struggling and fighting. They wanted peace and prosperity and were working hard to rebuild their country. Croatia's investment in infrastructure was and continues to be great, including an extensive modern highway system that allows you to travel through and across this mountainous country efficiently and comfortably thanks to a network of tunnels and bridges that is an engineering marvel. We like countries at turning points. They're lands of opportunity. That's how we perceived Croatia when we made our purchase there, meaning we believed an investment in real estate in that country at that time positioned us for long-term capital appreciation. The growing tourist markets in Croatia and especially in the region of Istria where we bought, thanks to annual film and truffles festivals, meant, as well, an opportunity for the property to generate cash flow when we weren't using it ourselves. Plus, we were buying in a country where real estate trades in euros, furthering our diversification agenda.

If your interest in investing in property overseas is not strictly and solely for cash flow but as much or maybe more to do with the allure of a second home in the sun or a pied-a-terre in a brand-name city, maybe you, like us in Istria years ago, have an idea about where you'd like to pursue those agendas—or maybe not. Maybe you're open to suggestions, looking for direction, and confused by all the choice.

If the agenda for your adventure overseas is driven more by your heart than your calculator, here are recommendations to help focus your thinking and further your plan. Following are glimpses into 18 countries where you could reinvent your life, full or part time, in retirement or otherwise, for the better, while diversifying your assets with the acquisition of a place of your own that could generate cash flow from rental when you're not using it yourself. I would classify these 18 countries as the world's top live-and-invest overseas havens. Each is, in its way and for different reasons, a great place to be.

Argentina

Late 2001, the Argentines removed the peg between their peso and the U.S. dollar, devaluing the Argentine currency, which fell, at its lowest point, to 4:1 against the greenback. This crisis situation opened a window of opportunity that we took advantage of to buy, in 2002, with friends, two classic-style apartments in Recoleta, one of the best addresses in the center of Buenos Aires, for half what the place would have been valued at prior to the devaluation debacle. We rented out the apartment for six years, used it occasionally ourselves, and then sold it, in 2008, to double our investment. Prices had returned to where they had been just before the previous collapse. We sold, coincidentally, near a top.

When speaking of Argentina, it's safer to refer to "a" top, rather than "the" top, as there have been many and will be many more. Bottoms, too, and we are, now, in fact, on the doorstep of another bottom. Argentina is a diverse country with lots of natural resources. It could be—should be—an economic success story, and, now and then, it is. It's also a case study in economic mismanagement on a colossal scale. The ongoing problem is politics, which keep this country in a perpetual cycle of crisis that make living in Argentina anything but dull. *Porteños* (the folks living in Buenos Aires) are uncommonly likely to seek regular psychotherapy, to undergo cosmetic surgery, and (alas) to commit suicide. Argentines are a kooky bunch. They enjoy the drama of their country, and, frankly, so do we. Like the people who live there, Buenos Aires is vibrant and full of personality. Visit this city and you will remember it always, and Buenos Aires is only the beginning of what Argentina has to offer.

Argentina makes about one-half of all the wine produced annually in South America. About half of this comes from Argentina's Mendoza region, where the landscapes of red earth and purple grapes appear eternal. Argentina's is a café culture, meaning the people value good wine, good coffee, and good conversation. The art of conversation, so alive here, could be part of the explanation for how the extremely varied Argentine population has managed to live harmoniously throughout history, despite the near constant influx and influence of immigrants, starting with the Spanish, who came in the quest for silver (*argentums* is Latin for silver). Argentina was a Spanish colony until 1816. Then came the Swiss, the Italians, and the French, who arrived with their grapes. The British arrived about this time, too, and administered the building of the country's infrastructure, including its national banking and large railway systems. In fact, trains still travel on the left-hand side of track, a last stand of British influence.

Argentina can be an ideal option for part-year living, as Argentina enjoys reverse seasons of those in the United States. The expat community is not overwhelming. You can tap into it if you'd like, for friends and support, or you can make your own way among the Argentines, who are friendly, polite, and respectful. Family is a priority, yet Argentines like to socialize. In Buenos Aires you have access to tango halls, live theater, antique fairs, art galleries, opera, ballet, symphony, and independent film festivals. Elsewhere in this enormous country is some of the best skiing and hiking in the world.

Argentina offers strong lifestyle choices, from Buenos Aires to Mendoza, but thanks to the high inflation of the recent years, it is not cheap right now. The cost of living is not a bargain, but real estate can be if you find a motivated seller. As the ongoing economic crisis continues, these are ever easier to come by.

Belize

Warm, welcoming, independent, and private —those four seemingly contradictory adjectives best describe both Belizeans and their country. Belize is also one of the safest countries in the world, despite what you may read about it. In some neighborhoods of Belize City, gang members and drug dealers do the things that gang members and drug dealers do, but those are small, contained areas. Outside Belize City, crime is nearly nonexistent, and this country's Cayo District could be one of the safest places in the world.

Belize was a colony of Britain until 1981, meaning the people here speak English. They also value their freedom, as it's relatively new.

In the nearly 30 years that Kathleen has been spending time in this country, she has joked that "the good news from Belize is no news from Belize." This is a sleepy Caribbean nation with but 330,000 people and three highways. On the other hand, little Belize offers a whole lot of what many retirees and investors are looking for—a chance to start over on sandy, sunny shores. Prices for a bit of sand on Ambergris, the most developed of Belize's islands, are not cheap but can be cheaper than elsewhere in the Caribbean. Other areas to shop in this country for the beach life are Placencia, on the southern mainland coast, and Corozal, on the northern mainland coast, where you're most likely to find a seaside bargain. We favor the interior Cayo region with its Mayan ruins, caves, rivers, waterfalls, and rain forest, a frontier where self-sufficient communities are emerging and attracting like-minded folks interested in being "independent together," as a friend living in this part of the world describes it.

Belize is a small country with a small population. You'll enjoy it here if you like wide-open spaces and small-town living where everyone knows everyone. You won't like it here if you crave regular doses of culture or First World–style amenities and services. With the exception of Ambergris Caye, where the country's biggest expat community is centered and where, as a result, services to cater to foreign retirees and investors have developed, life in Belize is best described as back-to-basics. There's not a single fast-food franchise or chain store in the entire country.

Legal residency is easy to obtain in Belize, and foreign residents pay no tax in Belize on non-Belize income. We would not recommend Belize if you have a serious health concern or existing medical condition. Healthcare facilities and standards are improving but limited.

Brazil

Brazil is one of the hemisphere's powerhouse economies, with a strongly emerging middle class. The country is energy-independent, has a solid industrial base, and is quickly becoming a world leader. Former President Lula da Silva's economic policies get much of the credit for Brazil's current enviable situation. According to the International Monetary Fund (IMF), per-capita income in Brazil rose by a staggering 162.8% between 2001 and 2010. During da Silva's tenure, the income of the richest Brazilians rose by 10%, while the income of the poorest Brazilians rose a hefty 72%. This has had a hugely positive economic impact. Today, Brazil's is the largest economy in South America and the eighth largest in the world.

Brazil's history is one of the Americas' fascinating stories. Over the years, it was the New World's great plantation slave society, host to its first major gold rush, and the country ruled by the hemisphere's only empire. Brazil was settled by the Dutch, the French, and the Portuguese, and, although the Portuguese ultimately gained control, all three left their cultural footprints, as did the Africans who came in slavery.

Brazil is an expansive country, but most of the viable lifestyle options are along the coast, from big city Rio de Janeiro to smaller beach towns like Florianopolis. We'd recommend taking a look at Maceió. The first Europeans to arrive here were Dutch settlers, who came to Brazil to start a sugar plantation to supply the ever-increasing demand in Europe in the early 1600s. The Portuguese took control of the area in the 1650s, and the city continued to grow. Maceió soon became a major seaport, exporting timber, tobacco, coconuts, leather, and spices.

Today, Maceió is modern, clean, and elegant with miles of white-sand beaches studded with colorful umbrellas and bordered by tall, swaying palms. Its warm turquoise waters gently lap the shores as beachgoers from all over enjoy the sun and sand. The town's long stretch of beachfront is the main attraction, and it's one of the best you'll find in Brazil. It's as naturally beautiful as it's possible for a beach to be, but without the bothersome vendors, beggars, and obvious sex trade that you'll find in other, better-known Brazilian beach cities. If you're in the market for cheap beachfront property, Maceió should be near the top of your list.

Downsides to Brazil include the small English-speaking population (relative to the 200 million inhabitants), meaning you'd have to learn Portuguese to make a success of living or investing in this country. Other downsides have to do with currency exchange rates and controls, important topics that we address in Part IV.

It used to be that Americans needed a visa to visit Brazil that had to be obtained prior to arriving in the country. This changed in 2019. Today, no visa is required unless you are visiting with the intention of establishing residency.

Chile

With its modern four-lane highways, reliable communications, and high standard of living, Chile can be one of Latin America's easiest transitions for American expats and retirees. If not completely First World, it is not far off the mark with the highest gross domestic product per capita in Latin America. The country feels efficient, well run, and safe. Utilities work, buses leave on time, and you can stroll the streets without worry. According to Transparency International, Chile is also one of the least corrupt countries in the Western Hemisphere, ranking slightly behind the United States.

The American Baby Boomer's introduction to Chile was the overthrow of President Salvador Allende in 1973. The aftermath of this event, the long, harsh dictatorship of General Augusto Pinochet, proved a greater shock to Chileans than everyone else. It was largely out of character with this nation's history. Chile today is peaceful, stable, and prosperous.

Santiago, Chile's capital city, was established by Spanish conquistador Pedro de Valdivia in 1540. Over the next decade, Valdivia expanded the colony in Chile, founding La Serena in 1544. It is this town we suggest you consider. Santiago is a great and modern city, but the extraordinarily high levels of pollution can make it an uncomfortable place to be. In La Serena, the skies are clear, with little pollution. At night the Milky Way lays a wide swath of glittering light across the skies, clearer here than practically anywhere else on Earth. For that reason, several major observatories are located in and near La Serena. The scientists who work at these facilities and their families make up a significant part of La Serena's expat community.

La Serena is a coastal community yet more temperate than tropical. Temperatures are pleasant year-round. This would not be a supercheap option but affordable and a good example of getting what you pay for. Chile in general, and La Serena in particular, offer a near-First World lifestyle for less overall than you'd pay in North America or Europe. The best value in La Serena is the cost of real estate. You can buy on the Pacific coast here for roughly one-quarter the cost of owning on the coast of California. One expat we know with experience in La Serena equates it to "California 40 years ago."

Colombia

Years ago, Kathleen sat around a table in a just-opened restaurant in a little-known mountain town in Panama called Boquete with a group of investors and businesspeople, in the country, as she was, to scout opportunity. "I believe that the potential in this place for retirees is enormous," one of the gentlemen in the group (the one who had just invested in opening the restaurant where we were having dinner) theorized. "Right now, the opportunity here is for the investor and the speculator. Property prices are so undervalued. Apartments in Panama City are a screaming bargain on a global scale. Pacific beachfront, Caribbean, farmland, riverfront, this country has it all, and it's all cheap.

"Panama is still misunderstood, suffering from a lingering case of bad press," the host for the evening continued. "When you say 'Panama' to an American today, he thinks: Noriega … drug cartels … CIA intrigue. It won't be too many years before those perceptions are flipped on their head. I predict that, five, seven years from now, when you say 'Panama' to the average American, he'll think: Retirement. Because that's what this country is gearing up to offer—a very appealing retirement option."

That was 1999. In August 2010, the AARP named Boquete, Panama, one of the top five places in the world to retire.

In 2011, we sat around a table in a just-opened restaurant in a little-known mountain town in Colombia called Medellín with a group of investors and businesspeople, in the country, as we were, to explore current opportunity. "Property values in this city are so undervalued," one of the gentlemen having dinner with us remarked. "I believe that apartment costs here are the lowest for any cosmopolitan city in the world on a per-square-meter basis. This is because Colombia, including Medellín, is still misunderstood. When you say 'Medellín' to the average American, he thinks: Drugs … gangs … Pablo Escobar. It's such a misperception. The current reality of this city is so far removed from all that."

Our host for the evening had just toured us around central Medellín, taking us to see apartment buildings he was rehabbing, converting into rentals, including one in a neighborhood we'd not visited before. "Manhattan retro chic" might be the best way to describe it. Running off a carefully maintained, beautifully landscaped park, these few side streets are lined with small colonial structures housing sushi restaurants, funky bars, contemporary art galleries, and vintage clothing and furniture shops. The last thing we felt was unsafe.

Prices have appreciated steadily in Medellín since that 2011 visit. At the same time, the U.S. dollar has gained steadily on the Colombian peso meaning that it's still possible to find good buys in dollar terms, and this city of springtime, flowers, and innovative urban planning remains one of our personal favorite places to be.

Like Brazil, Colombia imposes exchange controls, which should not put you off buying here, but they need to be understood and respected. Also, taxes are high.

Croatia

Neckties and wine. Croatia may be better known for its long coast along the sparkling green Adriatic and its tumultuous, 1,000-year-long history, but when we think of Croatia, we think of neckties and wine. This gorgeous, complicated country is the birthplace of both the necktie and the Zinfandel grape, and these two facts reveal a lot about Croatia. First, it has great weather. The Zinfandel grape requires a climate not too hot and not too cold. Croatia's mild winters and sunny summers make for perfect Zinfandel grape growing.

Second, Croats are the trendsetters credited with introducing today's tie to the fashion world. The Croat contingency of the French service wore their traditional knotted handkerchiefs during the Thirty Years' War (1618–1648). The Parisians took a fancy to them and called them *cravat*—a cross between the Croatian and French words for Croat (Hrvati and Croates). So began a cravat fashion frenzy. In the seventeenth century, these kerchiefs became so intricate that they were tied in place by strings and arranged in a bow that took forever to arrange.

Croatia is tucked into southeastern Europe, bordering the Adriatic Sea, between Bosnia, Herzegovina, and Slovenia. It's near the coast, Vienna, Venice, Budapest, skiing in Austria, and golf in Slovenia. It's been more than 20 years since the Socialist Federal Republic of Yugoslavia was dissolved. Its six republics—Croatia, Bosnia and Herzegovina, Macedonia, Montenegro, Serbia, and Slovenia—are all very much their own countries today. Croatia is wearing its new skin comfortably, as it should. The Kingdom of Croatia was, in fact, its own entity starting in 925 AD. It joined Hungary in 1102 but maintained a Croat culture with hopes for independence. Although it was titled a free royal town in 1242, it took about 800 years before Croatia was independent again, this time from Austria-Hungary in 1918. That freedom, too, was short-lived, however. Croatia became a member of Yugoslavia after World War II and didn't stand on its own again until 1992.

A Croatian friend told us a story about his family once. "My father lived to be more than 100 years old," Lovorko explained. "He lived his whole life in Croatia, here in Istria. Not only in the same town where he'd been born but in the same house. And, in his lifetime, he lived in nine different countries."

You have two strong lifestyle options in Croatia—the coast and the Istrian peninsula. The Adriatic waters offshore from Croatia are a sailor's paradise. Inland, in Istria, is a wonderland of another kind, with vineyards and olive groves. If you've any romance in your soul, we defy you not to fall in love with this country. The ancient Romans called it Terra Magica, the Magic Land. Perhaps the best part is that, unlike Tuscany—the region of Italy that Istria is most often compared with (with good reason, as the geography and the history of these two regions have much in common)—the average person can afford Istria, where you can buy a small, renovated cottage with lookouts over a valley and vineyards, perfect for regular visits, for rental, and for retirement, for as little as $100,000.

Retiring to Croatia, you'd be in good company. Diocletian, the only Roman emperor to abdicate his position (that is, to retire) was also the first person to retire overseas. Diocletian built a palace on the Dalmatian coast (his birthplace was Dalmatia), the location of current-day Split, and it is here, with the glorious Adriatic Sea spread out before him, that he chose to live out his days.

Dominican Republic

The Dominican Republic is an internationally popular all-inclusive resort destination that sees big volumes of tourists every year, thanks to its miles of sandy beaches and balmy temperatures. Indeed, 20% of all tourists to the Caribbean are headed to these shores specifically.

The Dominican Republic is also a top Caribbean choice for the would-be foreign-property investor and retiree. All that tourist infrastructure amounts to an extensive network of businesses and services that you can easily plug into, and, as a property owner or retiree on this island, you have more choices for the kinds of amenities you might be looking for than you'll typically find elsewhere in this part of the world.

Expats have been coming to the Dominican Republic, starting businesses and launching services geared toward their fellow foreign residents, for four decades. In the Samana Peninsula, for example, on the Dominican Republic's northeast coast, French and Italian food brands line the shelves of the expat-run specialty grocery stores, and signs for businesses are in English, French, Italian, and Spanish. Foreigners do not get curious looks, because there are so many of them. The locals have enjoyed friendly relations with these settlers for a long time.

We'd say Las Terrenas, on the Samaná Peninsula, offers the best lifestyle in the country. What sets Las Terrenas apart in the DR—and from any other beach town in the region—is its sophisticated lifestyle. The French settled Las Terrenas generations ago, and their mark is clear. People greet each other with kisses on both cheeks, signs are in French, and baguette is de rigueur.

Harder to explain are the local property prices—figures that would be unheard of in most other parts of the Caribbean. You can buy a condo close to one of Las Terrenas' most beautiful beaches for less than $100,000. Villas start from under $200,000. And, if you'd prefer to build your own dream home, ocean-view lots are available for as little as $30 to $40 a square meter, and building packages for a two-bedroom villa start from $160,000. Rental returns on the best beachfront units are in the range of 9% to 12% net.

The Dominican Republic is easily accessible, especially from the East Coast of the United States, and offers competitive residency options. On the other hand, despite the established expat communities and the products and services they provide, this is a Third World country with Third World hassles and frustrations. It's also a Caribbean island in the hurricane zone.

Ecuador

Lots of overseas retirement destinations tout the fact that they're just like the United States, that, retired there, you could settle in to familiar surroundings. You won't hear that about Ecuador. Each day you spend in this country, you know you're in a different and wonderful part of the planet.

Ecuador is also the world's best place to retire overseas on a budget and to live better for less. The cost of living is low, and the cost of real estate is near rock bottom for Latin America. The healthcare is high quality, honest, and inexpensive. Specifically, we recommend Cuenca, Ecuador, a beautiful Spanish-colonial city with a fresh, spring-like climate 12 months of the year and a large and growing expat community that is one of Latin America's most diverse and well blended.

Cuenca's historic center measures roughly 12 by 20 blocks, big enough but manageable. Most of the streets are of cobblestone and hemmed in by Spanish-colonial buildings that seldom exceed three stories. Downtown Cuenca is generally well preserved, considering the original adobe construction, and today's Cuenca boasts cafes, restaurants, bars, and bookshops alongside traditional butchers, tailors, repair shops, clothing stores, and bakeries. The city is built around its beautiful town square, anchored by the original cathedral at one end (built 1557) and the "new" cathedral (1800s) at the other. Ecuador has other colonial cities, but Cuenca is the cultural heart of the country, with an orchestra and active art, theater, even tango traditions that you can often enjoy free.

Perhaps the biggest draw to Cuenca is its cost of living, which is low in an absolute sense. And living here you don't have to worry about currency exchange rates affecting your cost of living adversely; Ecuador uses the US dollar. Real estate, too, is an absolute bargain. You can buy a city condo for less than $100,000. The city's premium location is the historic center; this is the area that should hold its value even in the face of market ups and downs. It's a recognized world treasure.

While Cuenca is a developed city, much of Ecuador is not, with poor though improving infrastructure. Ecuador has the highest population density in South America (about 55 people per square kilometer) with a high percentage of indigenous and mestizos. This means we gringos stand out. If you want to blend in with the locals, you'd be more comfortable in another destination.

France

France has a polarizing effect on Americans. We either love the place or we hate it, and many of us believe the French hate us back. That last part is wholly untrue in our experience. It's also not true that the French are rude. They're among the mostwell-mannered people we've come across anywhere.

Whenever readers of our e-letters ask for our recommendation for the best place in the world to live or retire, budget considerations notwithstanding, we say France. It's the world's best example of getting what you pay for. There are reasons France sees more tourists than any other country in the world, some 90 million of them annually, which is 30% greater volume than the country's own permanent population. To accommodate all those tourists, the infrastructure of this country, from the airports and the train system to the restaurants to the hotels, has to be top notch and is.

France is not only perhaps the best place in the world to live, thanks to its food, wine, architecture, history, museums, parks, gardens, and cultural and recreational offerings, but it's also, thanks to its reliable tourist trade, one of the best places to think about buying for cash flow. A rental property in France, especially in Paris but elsewhere in the country, too, is about as recession-proof a cash-flowing investment as you're going to find.

France would never feature on a list of the world's bargain destinations; still, outside Paris, this country can be more affordable than you might imagine and even Paris doesn't have to be hyperexpensive. Much of the best it has to offer comes free (the parks, gardens, river walks, and most museums at least one day per month). But France isn't about cost of living; it's about quality of life. Paris is the most beautiful, most romantic place on earth, and France has much to offer beyond its City of Light. It can be possible to own your own piece of French country life for less than $100,000, especially if you're up for a renovation project.

Downsides to France include the bureaucracy. Thanks to Napoleon, all Civil Law countries love their paperwork, but, as ground zero for the Napoleonic Code, the French are best at this game. You can get almost anything done in this country if you have a paper stamped by some government official saying it's okay. It's getting that stamp that can leave you panting and ranting.

Ireland

We arrived on the Emerald Isle with our little family and our business expecting to plug into the kind of infrastructure we were used to back in the United States. That didn't happen because the kind of infrastructure we take for granted in the States (related to transportation, telecommunications, banking, credit, etc.) doesn't exist in Ireland. Trying to run a business in this country, we felt like we were continually banging our heads against an Irish stone wall. Finally, frustrated and confused, we had to admit that we weren't going to change how the Irish lived and did business. We'd have to go along. We had no choice.

Now, years later, we find ourselves increasingly homesick for this country. With age and time, our perspective has shifted.

One day, after we'd been living in Waterford for maybe three years, a couple of readers stopped by our office. They were Indians, in the country to investigate the possibilities for relocating their software company from India to Ireland. Did we have any advice for them, they wanted to know. The couple represented the contradiction of the day. The Celtic Tiger was roaring loud, attracting investors (like us) from far and wide, entrepreneurs and businesspeople looking for opportunity, but we were all misguided. Ireland was holding out great opportunity, but not of the kind we were in the market for at the time, and that young Indian couple was confused when I warned them away. "Don't come to Ireland to run a business," I told them. "You'll be driven mad."

That advice is probably much less valid today but, more important, it misses the point. We lived in this country during the apex of the Celtic Tiger, which generated great amounts of wealth, more money than this island had ever known. As a result, the Irish then, like us, were distracted from what was right in front of them. They were busy covering their ancient green land with suburban tract homes, shopping malls, and fast-food franchises. We watched as pubs were replaced by nightclubs and as car dealerships eventually kept Saturday business hours and banks finally remained open through lunch. Ireland wanted so badly to compete on the global business stage. In that regard, it failed completely.

But now, when we think of our time in Waterford, the things that come to mind have nothing to do with business. We remember the owner of the corner shop across the street from our office and how he and his wife sent us a small gift when Jackson was born and inquired after both Jackson and his big sister Kaitlin every time we saw them. We remember the cabinet-maker who helped to restore our big old Georgian house to its original glories, shutter by shutter, wood plank by wood plank. We think of the castles and the gardens we explored on weekends and the few times we braved the beaches at Tramore, sitting on the sand in sweaters, shivering and shaking our heads, while, out in the cold Irish Sea, the Irish swam and surfed. We remember cows blocking the roads and sheep dotting the green fields. These are the pictures of Ireland we carry now.

The surest bets for rental purchase are the tourist trails—the Ring of Kerry, the southwest coast, Galway, and Dublin. Pay attention to proximity to amenities that are important to renters—the ocean, a nearby airport so they can hop around Europe, and a town they can walk to rather than having to drive (remember, the Irish drive on the left).

Ireland is less appealing as a place to retire these days since it changed its laws related to the requirements for establishing residency. Now you need to prove income of at least 50,000 euro per person per year to qualify.

Italy

"BARGAIN! Independent house, 110 square meters on two floors, composed of living room with fireplace, large kitchen, two bedrooms, bathroom. Private garden of 2,000 square meters. Good condition, recently restored. 75,000 euro."

That's a recent listing for a house in Italy. Not in Tuscany or Umbria but a corner of Italy that I'd say is at least as lovely. The beaches are golden, and the sea rolls out like a giant bolt of turquoise silk. Stitching together seascapes with lush mountain valleys, this region is one of Italy's secret treasures. You can have the best of all worlds here at prices a fraction of those in this country's more discovered regions. If your budget is small, you can still afford Italy, if you opt for Abruzzo. Real estate here is up to 80% cheaper than in Tuscany and up to 50% cheaper than in Umbria.

You know the appeals of Italy, but you may not realize the diversity of lifestyles on offer in this country. On my most recent visit to Italy with the kids, we made a stab at recreating a version of the Grand Tour of old, exploring Italy's most heralded destinations with an eye to answering the question in each case, would we want to buy real estate or live here?

Venice is a gem of a place that you should see if you can. To be happy living here, you'd have to enjoy life on the water (getting anywhere requires a ferry or boat ride). I'd find it a hassle after a while. Certainly you'd want to leave in summer, when the temperatures can top 35 degrees Celsius for days on end and the narrow streets of this lagoon city are overrun with camera-toting hordes. In winter, the tourists are mostly gone, but the days are cold and damp. The real reason, though, why Venice isn't a top choice is its cost of living. Real estate values can exceed those of Paris (5,000 euro per square meter in out-of-the-way places to 20,000 euro and more per square meter overlooking the Grand Canal).

Ravenna is a stark contrast. This is a quiet Italian village with a rich history that today is largely overlooked. We made a point of stopping here because our art historian daughter wanted to see Justinian's mosaic in the Basilica of San Vitale. While in Venice, the queue for the basilica was hours long, in Ravenna, we walked straight up to the window, bought our tickets, and continued directly into the church, where we had no competition at all for front-row viewing of the ancient masterpiece. The heart of Ravenna's old town is interesting and pleasant but small. Overall, that's the trouble with this city—too small. What would you do here after you'd viewed the noteworthy art and architecture? On the other hand, lunch in Ravenna cost less than 10 euro per head, whereas the best you'll do in Venice will be more than double that.

Rome isn't small, and, living there, you'd never run out of fun and interesting ways to spend your time. On the other hand, Rome is urban without the veneer that Paris has managed to paint over herself. Whereas Paris (to continue the comparison) is genteel and romantic, Rome is gritty and real. That said, Rome could be a much more affordable place to live than Paris. Avoid the tourist zones (as you would as a resident), and you could enjoy a full life here on an average budget.

One of Italy's biggest surprises is Pisa. Everyone comes to see the tower, but Pisa offers more. Its riverfront homes, candy-striped basilica, and baptistery showcase a bygone age of wealth. At one time, Pisa merchants competed successfully with those of Venice. Eventually, the city fell to Florence. Today, it's a one-hour stop for tour buses, but if you're looking for an Old World lifestyle, I'd give this city more attention. The old town is charming, and the town beyond is pleasant. There's enough here to keep your interest and to support a fully appointed life on the Continent, and you're minutes from the sea. Whereas Venice, Rome, and Florence are given over entirely to tourists each season, Pisa is quiet year-round. Busloads of travelers come and go from the tower each day while the rest of the city goes about its business. Because few seem to recognize any reason to stick around, real estate can be a bargain. You could buy a one-bedroom apartment here for as little as 200,000 euro.

If you're an art lover, Florence may seem like heaven, and, indeed, there's much in Florence to keep you occupied and engaged, but, to me, it doesn't feel like a place to call home. While Pisa is cozy, Florence is aloof. Florence would also be a dramatically more expensive choice. Better, maybe, to base yourself in Pisa and visit Michelangelo's hometown. It's but an hour away via *autostrade*.

Malaysia

Showing the bias of our perspective, we refer to Malaysia as Asia's Panama. That is to say, this country is a regional and a global hub, for trade, for business, and for cultures. The cost of living is affordable, although elsewhere in Asia (Thailand, Vietnam, China) can be cheaper. Kuala Lumpur (KL), Malaysia's capital, is clean, efficient, and well functioning, with shopping, restaurants, and all the other trappings of a modern metropolis. It's also (again like Panama) an expat melting pot with big numbers of expats both from all over Asia and, to a lesser extent, the West. Malaysia is more welcoming of foreigners than any other country in Asia. Its My Second Home program makes retiree residency easy to obtain, meaning you don't have to worry about regular "border runs," as many expats in this part of the world do. Because it is a former British colony, English is widely spoken, so you don't have to worry about trying to learn to speak Malay either.

Kuala Lumpur, located in the heart of the Malaysian peninsula, is a city of contrasts. The shining stainless-steel Petronas Towers, two of the tallest skyscrapers in the world, anchor a startlingly beautiful and unique skyline. Modern, air-conditioned malls flourish, selling everything from batik clothing to genuine Rolex watches and Tiffany jewelry. In the shadows of these ultra-modern buildings, the ancient Malay village of Kampung Baru still thrives, with free-roaming roosters and a slow pace of life generally found in rural villages. Less than a 20-minute walk from the city center, you can find yourself in the company of monkeys.

Life is different here than in the West. When you go to your neighborhood shop, take your time and converse with the owner, ask about his family as he asks you about yours. By the second or third time you visit, you are recognized and waved to when you walk down the sidewalk. You may be invited to dinner or at least to share a cup of rich *kopi*. In some Asian cities, it's easy for a foreigner to feel something akin to a walking wallet. Not in KL. Foreigners pay the same prices as the locals. Health care is first-rate, public transportation is modern and efficient, and the tap water is safe to drink. Beautiful beaches are just a short drive or flight away, cool mountain retreats can be reached in less than an hour, and the thriving city-state of Singapore is easily accessible in a few hours by car, train, or bus or an hour by plane.

Although KL is more expensive than rural Malaysia, it is marvelously inexpensive by Western standards. You could realistically expect to cut your living expenses by a third and still enjoy a lifestyle comparable to what you are accustomed to now. If Asia interests you, this is one place where you could pursue the ultimate diversification strategy. That is, while Malaysia, like all Asia, imposes restrictions on foreign ownership of land, you could purchase a house or an apartment in this country that could work for personal use, retirement, and rental. This is why Malaysia is the only Asian destination we've chosen to highlight.

Mexico

Mexico is a big place with a bad reputation. The reputation isn't altogether undeserved, as drug cartels do control parts of this country but not all of it, and some of the most appealing regions for both living and investing sit outside the war zones. Mexico offers two long coasts, mountain towns, and colonial cities, plus Mayan ruins, jungle, rain forest, rivers, and lakes. It's also the most accessible "overseas" haven from the United States. You could drive back and forth if you wanted.

For all these reasons, Mexico is home to the biggest established populations of American expats in the world, making it a great choice if you seek adventure with the comforts of home. Mexico is no longer a supercheap option, but it is my top pick for enjoying a luxury coastal lifestyle on a budget, in Puerto Vallarta. Puerto Vallarta is more expensive than other places where you might consider living or retiring overseas, but in Puerto Vallarta that's not the point. This isn't developing-world living. This stretch of Mexico's Pacific coastline has already been developed to a high level. Life here can be not only comfortable but also easy and fully appointed. In Puerto Vallarta, you aren't buying for someday, as you can be in many coastal destinations in Central America. In Puerto Vallarta, you can buy a world-class lifestyle in a region with world-class beaches and ocean views that is supported, right now, by world-class golf courses, marinas, restaurants, and shopping. This is a lifestyle that is available only on a limited basis worldwide, a lifestyle that is truly (not metaphorically) comparable to the best you could enjoy in southern California if you could afford it. Here you can afford it even on an average budget.

Real estate options in Puerto Vallarta vary from modest to jet set, in terms of both products available and price points. You could buy a small apartment outside Puerto Vallarta town for less than $100,000, or you could buy big and fancy for $1 million-plus. Whatever you buy, you could rent it out when you're not using it. The Puerto Vallarta region, including the emerging Riviera Nayarit that runs north from it along the coast, is a tourist rental market with a track record.

The other spot in Mexico worth highlighting is Ajijic and Lake Chapala, in the mountains, one of the largest and most established expatriate communities in the world. Ajijic, less than an hour from Guadalajara, has been attracting retirees for decades thanks to its lake (despite the lake's on-and-off environmental problems) and cool weather. Again, you could buy here, small and modest, for less than $100,000.

Nicaragua

Nicaragua was once the breadbasket of Central America. Thanks to the first round of Sandinista rule and the confiscation of farmland in the name of "the people," that changed in the 1980s. The activities of the Sandinistas also created a stigma related to property rights in this country that remains. The country's current Sandinista President Daniel Ortega, however, hasn't done anything to infringe on anyone's property rights, but he is keeping both foreign investors and tourists away, meaning values are seriously depressed.

Geographically, Nicaragua is blessed, with two long coastlines and two big lakes, plus volcanoes, highlands, rain forest, and rivers. In this regard, it's got everything Costa Rica and Panama have got, all less discovered and developed and available for the adventurer and eco-traveler at bargain rates. Architecturally, too, Nicaragua is notable. Its two sister colonial cities, Granada and Leon, vie for the title of Oldest City in the Americas. Whichever story you believe (that the Spanish conquistadores settled first on the shores of Lake Nicaragua at Granada or, perhaps, a few months earlier in Old Leon), Nicaragua is the big winner, with impressive colonial-era churches, public buildings, and parks to her credit.

Recent protests related to proposed changes to the country's pension programs and the ongoing general concern over what trouble Ortega might get up to have created a crisis investment opportunity in a country that, its political and economic troubles notwithstanding, we continue to find appealing. You wouldn't be buying confident of appreciating values or reliable rental returns, but, if you appreciate the country's beauty, history, and people, as we do, this is a chance to take a position among them for pennies on the dollar.

Panama

Panama has been one of the world's most important crossroads since the days when pirates ruled these waters. You name it, it passes through Panama in some way at some time going somewhere. Largely as a result of its crossroads positioning but also thanks to its reputation worldwide as a top retirement, tax, and business haven, Panama is the fastest-growing market in the region and one of the fastest-growing countries in the world.

Panama's benefits are many, including First World health care at Third World prices and the world's gold standard program of special benefits for retirees (plus 14 resident visa options for the nonretiree). It's also one of the world's few remaining tax havens (meaning you can operate an online business here tax-free), and a U.S. dollar-based economy (meaning zero currency risk for dollar holders).

When the United States handed over operations of the Panama Canal to the Panamanians, and the 10,000 U.S. military and their families departed the Canal Zone in 1999, the country fell into recession. A lot of disposable income disappeared overnight. Panama worked quickly to find ways to replace the lost economic activity. One focus since has been attracting the foreign-retiree market. In addition, the country has developed its tourism, banking, and financial-services industries and has invested in the expansion of its canal, which generates more than $2.6 billion annually. That's a lot of cash flow for a country of about 4.3 million people.

Panama is a small country but offers many lifestyle and investment options, some better than others. Panama City is not a top lifestyle choice but, thanks to all the foreign business and investment activity, the best place in the country to buy for reliable cash flow and value appreciation long term. Certainly you should be able to resell it easily when you're ready; this is about as liquid a market as you'll find. The best buy outside the capital is Pacific beachfront. The farther from Panama City, the better the price.

Portugal

Have you ever wondered why Portugal is at the center of the world map? It's because the Portuguese were the first to map the world.

"We have a word in Portuguese," a friend from Lisbon, Miguel, told us once, "that doesn't exist in any other language.

"The word is *saudade*. It means a longing for, a missing or a yearning for something. It's a noun, not a verb, and its meaning is born from the feeling of a young wife for her husband sailor long at sea."

"Yes, and this is connected to another important word for us," another friend, João, interjected. "*Saudade* is connected to *fado*.

"*Fado* is our traditional music, but it is also our destiny. It is not good, it is not bad. It is simply the way your life is because of the choices you have made."

"Yes," Miguel explained. "*Saudade* is the *fado* of the woman who has chosen to marry a sailor. It comes with the territory."

Most of the world looks at Portugal as the edge of Europe. The Portuguese look at the world map and see themselves right at the center, at the heart. Portugal identifies herself with the sea. For the Portuguese, the sea is part of their territory, a continuation of their domain. For them, therefore, Portugal is quite expansive.

In recent history, Portugal has been mostly ignored and overlooked, but there was a time when this country had the world's attention. It was the Portuguese Prince Henry the Navigator, an architect of the Age of Exploration, who bid his men to "sail on, sail on." Those orders compelled brave adventurers around the Cape of Good Hope to China and India and then across the Atlantic. Those orders were given, specifically, from the very bottom of the country's long Algarve coast, in Sagres, where Henry built his famous School of Navigation. It was from this point that Portuguese explorers set off to discover if indeed dragons lay beyond these shores. At the time, this was the acknowledged end of the world.

Portugal's Algarve region is a unique bit of European geography at the southwestern corner of the Continent, at the longitude of Great Britain and the latitude of Delaware. It is protected from winter by the movement of the ocean in the Gulf Stream, and, as a result, it has the best climate in Europe, with more sunny days than any other country in this part of the world and steady winds that mean the region is never unbearably hot and rarely humid.

Unlike many sunny paradises, the Algarve is not a little island in the middle of nowhere. It is attached to the Continent and reachable by car from Lisbon and points farther north. You can fly here from the U.S. East Coast in short hops, as few as six hours to Lisbon from Boston, for example, where many flights originate thanks to the Portuguese diaspora. From Lisbon, it's a three-hour drive or a quick flight to the Algarve coast.

Another reason the Algarve is such an appealing choice for North Americans seeking adventure, reinvention, opportunity, or a new life abroad is thanks to the British. The monarchs of Portugal and England married each other from the fourteenth century on, creating the oldest alliance in Europe before Europe really existed. The Anglo-Portuguese friendship did not end with the death of Prince Henry and his brothers. British royals carried on marrying Portuguese princesses. Then, after World War II, the Anglo-American allies continued to operate from the Azores, a Portuguese territory. Over time, as a result, many British families settled in Portugal. By the 1950s, they had begun to populate the southern coast. A decade or so later, the charms of the Algarve were discovered by the Beatles and their fans, who moved in to the fishing port town of Albufeira, still the home of the most authentic fish and chips in the region.

Despite all this attention from British tourists and expats, the Algarve was thankfully never as overbuilt as the Costa Brava in Spain for a practical reason. The terrain is too hilly to allow mass-produced ticky-tacky little boxes to be plunked down, as they have been, over the decades, along stretches of the Spanish coast.

The most important relic of all the years of close association with the British is one key to American and Canadian happiness in the Algarve today. Nearly everyone here speaks English—both the local population and the big non-British foreign population. It is the lingua franca for the region.

The Algarve offers a one-of-a-kind lifestyle that could be described at once as quintessential Old World and twenty-first-century resort and that represents one of the Continent's best values. This is a land of medieval towns, traditional fishing villages, open-air markets, cobblestoned streets, and whitewashed houses with lace-patterned chimneys surrounded by fig, olive, almond, and carob trees... all fringed by a 100-mile-long coastline that includes some of the best beaches in the world.

Portugal's Algarve checks all the boxes for the would-be traveler, expat, retiree, or property investor. It's safe and stable, beautiful and welcoming, healthy and affordable. It has great weather (with 3,300 hours of sunshine per year), top-notch infrastructure, and international-standard healthcare available for a very low cost. The region's 100 miles of coastline boast some of the best beaches in Europe and 42 golf courses. Portugal offers the most user-friendly and affordable residency option in the eurozone, and retirement income is not taxed. Real estate values have been rising since 2015, but you can still find great bargains relative to the rest of Western Europe.

Spain

If culture is a priority for you, look to Spain. History, architecture, literature, art, and music are part of daily life. Outdoors enthusiasts, too, will enjoy Spain. The Spanish coast is a golfer's paradise. However, in many other regards, this is one of the most overhyped and disappointing stretches of coastline in the world. The nicest thing that can be said about it is that it's ultracheap in the wake of this country's ongoing property market collapse.

Spain has become a traditional retirement destination for Europeans, like Arizona and Florida for Americans. You can find here, if you're interested, big expat retiree communities along the Mediterranean coast and smaller ones elsewhere. Or you could decide on one of the country's interesting cities, from Barcelona to Valencia or Seville. If you prefer a cooler climate, look at the country's north coast.

One spot in particular we would recommend is the Costa Tropical, one of the least-known, quietest, and most authentically Spanish of the Mediterranean *costas*. The Costa Tropical is in the province of Andalusia. It lies to the east of the infamous (and horrible) Costa del Sol and to the west of the desert-like Costa Almeria (Spaghetti Western country). The Costa Tropical's position between the brilliant blue Mediterranean and the soaring Sierra Nevada Mountains creates a subtropical climate where living things flourish. Attracting visitors for its climate, beaches, and scuba diving, it also makes a great base for exploring inland Andalusia and the beautifully preserved white villages of the Alpujarras, Granada's mesmerizing Alhambra Palace, and the Sierra Nevada National Park. Morocco is not far away.

Almuñécar (almoo-nyEAh-car), one of the Costa Tropical three main communities, combines the charm of a typical Spanish town with the best of northern European influences and services. The locals are open and friendly, and the expats are happy to be here. This town, with a population of 22,000, has hung on to its Spanish charm, unlike the better-known Spanish coastal towns, and tends to attract more Spanish than foreign visitors. The town has an incredibly wide range of historical influences, including Phoenician, Roman, and Moorish. "How could you live anywhere else?" asks the town's Mayor Don Juan Carlos Benavides, and he may have a point.

Uruguay

Uruguay is known the world over for the beautiful beaches running the entire length of its coast. The country's best value in beach property is the Costa de Oro, a 30-mile stretch of shoreline with uninterrupted golden sands whose name translates to the "golden coast." What's more, the Costa de Oro also contains some of Uruguay's best coastal towns for full-time retirement living. It offers something else, too, that most of the Atlantic coastline does not: incredible sunsets, thanks to the general east-west orientation of its shoreline.

Best of all, you're in Uruguay, a country that offers a peaceful, genuinely laid-back culture, along with a notable absence from the world's conflicts, and where expats can obtain easy residency and even a second passport. Uruguay has a solid financial center and an economy that continued to grow during the recent worldwide recession. It's also a country with abundant ground water, mild weather, and a surplus of renewable electricity from hydropower. All things considered, it is an appealing package—a beautiful coastline with First-World infrastructure, a solid democracy with a healthy financial system, and shady seaside towns where the beachfront homes start at just $75,000.

Uruguay is located on lower South America's eastern seaboard, wedged between Argentina and Brazil. The country shares a land border with Brazil and is separated from Argentina by a wide river, the Río de la Plata. The capital city of Montevideo, the southernmost capital in the Western

Hemisphere, is home to almost half of Uruguay's 3.5 million residents. Roughly the size of the American state of Missouri, Uruguay is the second-smallest country in South America after Suriname.

In the 1800s, the country's Costa de Oro was considered a worthless stretch of land. It consisted mostly of moving dunes, which in some places extended for miles inland from the sea. Two of the area's first development initiatives were dune-forestation projects at Atlántida and La Floresta, resulting in today's abundance of shady pines, eucalyptus, and sycamore trees in these spots. By 1910, the area was starting to get the attention of Montevideo's wealthy families who were looking for country getaways and seaside retreats. In the late 1930s, development increased dramatically as the first land subdivisions were planned. The area drew the attention of European investors looking for a sound place to invest outside Europe as World War II began. This stretch of coastline continued to be popular, attracting the elite of Montevideo and beyond, until the 1950s. Then the Punta del Este began to draw wealthy vacationers farther along the coast. The Costa de Oro's popularity is on the upswing again, as expats and second-home shoppers from North America are taking note of the excellent property values on offer.

Uruguay can qualify as sleepy, which can be a pro or a con, but never-sleepy Buenos Aires is only a quick flight or ferry ride away. The other potential downside to this country is the distance from North America and the fact that few flights serve Montevideo direct from the United States. You have more options connecting through Buenos Aires.

2

Cash Flow from Property Overseas Can Fund Your Dream Retirement

About 600,000 American retirees have their Social Security payments direct-deposited into foreign banks or receive their monthly checks at foreign addresses, and many thousands of retirees living overseas continue to have their Social Security payments deposited into U.S. bank accounts (because it's easier). In other words, there's no way to know for sure how many American retirees are retired beyond U.S. borders, but we can tell you one thing with certainty: the number is growing fast.

The current plight of the American retiree is well known. Baby Boomer retirees, having worked hard, invested in homes, raised families, and dreamed of the day it would all pay off, are right now facing the reality that things aren't playing out as they'd long hoped. Maybe their retirement account is worth less than what they expected it'd be worth at this point—if they have a retirement account at all. Nearly half of Americans 55 and older don't. Maybe their home is worth less than they were counting on, too, or, worse, they may owe more on their mortgage than the property could reasonably be expected to sell for. Maybe they, like almost 30% of Americans, have no emergency savings. Maybe, bottom line, their retirement resources aren't enough to fund the retirement they've been looking forward to or even to cover the bills.

If you're at or approaching this stage of life yourself, you understand the concerns, and you're likely worried, maybe panicked, over your future. How can you avoid giving up on your long-held dream retirement lifestyle? Thinking more practically, how can you make sure you don't outlive your retirement nest egg?

Retire overseas.

It's possible to retire comfortably in a number of beautiful, friendly, safe, pleasant destinations on a budget of $1,400 per month or less. Coincidentally, that's just about the amount of the average monthly Social Security check, meaning that it isn't exaggerating the point to say that it's possible for the average American to retire overseas on Social Security alone. It's also possible to retire in the United States on Social Security alone. It must be, because many Americans are doing it. The question is, what standard of living can the retiree afford on Social Security alone stateside, especially if his Social Security check amounts to but $1,400 or less each month? Generally speaking, the answer is: Not great.

This leads to the other primary reason to consider relocating abroad in retirement—to improve your quality of life. Dollar for dollar, the lifestyle your retirement budget could buy you in dozens of places around the world will be richer, fuller, and more interesting than the lifestyle that budget could buy you in the United States. Retiring overseas, this phase of life shifts from being a cause for concern to the adventure of your lifetime. We make this claim based on more than three decades of experience watching and helping thousands of Americans retire beyond their own borders.

Retiring to another country means moving completely outside your comfort zone. It requires an open mind, a ready sense of humor, and a willingness to accept, at this later stage of life, that you don't know everything and that you've still got much to learn. Retiring overseas means starting over. That's terrifying, maybe, but—ultimately and more importantly—it's also an opportunity for personal renaissance. Sure, your costs of housing and of health care will be reduced and you'll maybe be able to dine out as often as you like and afford to indulge in help around the house, but, more interesting big picture, retiring overseas also means that you're making new friends, forming a new circle of support, seeing new places, experiencing a new culture, and maybe learning a new language. At an age when others are considering returning to the workforce as Walmart greeters or Uber drivers in desperate attempts to pay their winter heating bills, you could be taking off for exotic, sun-drenched shores where heating is unnecessary any time of year.

A migration is taking place. It began quietly on the fringes, perhaps three decades ago, but now it's building momentum and making its way onto mainstream America's radar. The Associated Press, the AARP, the *New York Times,* and *USA Today* have all reported on it. We call it the Retirement Revolution. If you're an investor, you can position yourself ahead of this mega-shift to profit in the markets these wandering retirees are making. If you're a retiree, you'd do well to think about joining the march.

The case for considering launching your retirement overseas is strong. That's not our point here. Our point is that, once you've decided to launch your retirement overseas, you're going to need a place to live wherever "overseas" turns out to be for you. In this context, you're not buying for investment. You're buying for retirement. As a retiree-buyer, your purchase decision should be led not by path-of-progress assessments, cash-flow projections, capital-return expectations, or currency movements, not by anything cognitive or quantifiable, but by your heart and your gut.

When a retiree decides to take his retirement global, one of the first big questions he or she faces is where? Not only where in the world (as in what country might be best for you), but also where to reside, as in a house? an apartment? a gated community? In fact, though, the question at first shouldn't be where to buy a retirement residence overseas. The question at first for the retiree-buyer should be: Should you *buy* a retirement residence overseas at all?

Owning Versus Renting

If your overseas real estate agenda is purely to do with finding a place to live in retirement in a foreign country, maybe it's not a real estate purchase you want—at least not right away—but a rental.

For each of our three international moves—from the United States to Waterford, Ireland; from Waterford to Paris; then from Paris to Panama City, Panama—we rented first and were glad we did. Because, in each case, we discovered that the place where we settled initially wasn't the place where we really wanted to be. In Waterford, we realized we didn't want to be in the city but outside it, so we could experience Irish country living. In Paris, it was a matter of a dozen blocks or so, but that distance made the difference between being at the heart of the chaos come tourist season each year and being hidden away and removed from it while still having the best of central Paris on our doorstep. In Panama City, we relocated three times before finally finding the neighborhood where we feel most comfortable.

Panama City is a good example, because, for a small city, the diversity of lifestyle options is great, and neighborhoods just a mile or two away from each other make for dramatically different living experiences. Buying before giving yourself a chance to understand this can mean the difference between loving your new life overseas and regretting it. Thinking more practically, depending on the country where you're retiring, the costs of buying and reselling property can be significant, meaning that buying wrong can be expensive.

On the other hand, we can imagine circumstances when you might choose to ignore our rent-first caveat and buy from the start of your retire overseas adventure. If you're retiring to a place where property values are appreciating, waiting a year before buying means you could be passing up healthy gains. Remember, the market dynamics that attracted you are attracting others, and early buyers enjoy the greatest rates of appreciation.

In addition, buying means creating the potential for cash flow from renting out your place when you're not using it.

Rent-Free Retirement

Buying real estate overseas is fundamentally about diversification. This is true whether you buy for investment or for retirement and argues in favor of buying for retirement rather than renting. Buying your new retirement residence overseas means moving money out of the United States and putting it into another market and, potentially, another currency. Moving all your money out of the States and into a new retirement residence overseas doesn't alone bring you the diversification you should be seeking right now. However, using some of your capital to purchase a retirement residence in the place where you want to live and putting other of your capital to work in another market (that perhaps uses a different currency) gets you not only diversification but also what amounts to a rent-free retirement.

Another advantage of buying your retirement residence overseas rather than renting it is that it helps you to "take the plunge." It allows you to move your life forward, unequivocally, embracing the new adventure. Many who rent before they buy do so to be able to maintain a property back home, "just in case." While this can be sensible, it's also an anchor, a drag. It can divide your attention and keep you looking backward instead of ahead to your new life. Keeping one foot on the pier and the other on the departing boat can land you in the drink. You may remain only partially committed, which will be a handicap.

The bottom line for the retiree buyers is to follow your instincts, not only with regards to what to buy overseas but also when answering the question, should you buy at all? You know yourself, your motivations and preferences, and how well you've researched your chosen destination. You know your level of commitment, your level of readiness, and your tolerance for risk.

Lee's Overseas Retirement Adventure

A friend, Lee, took early retirement at the age of 49 from a successful engineering career based in Manhattan and moved first to Ecuador, then to Uruguay, next to Brazil, then Colombia, and, most recently, last year, to Mexico. In each case, Lee bought a home, and, in each case, he was rewarded. A significant part of Lee's income over the past 18 years of his retirement has come from his serial home ownership in each of the countries where he's been retired.

"I didn't have enough of a pension or enough retirement savings to live on for the rest of my life in the States, certainly not living the level of lifestyle my wife and I had been enjoying in New York up until that point," Lee explains. "So I started looking around for options. My eyes were opened to the 'retire overseas' option by a book on retiring to Costa Rica that I happened upon in a bookstore one day. At that point in our lives, my wife Julie and I wanted a big change, an adventure. We craved culture shock, the bigger the better. So, while Costa Rica was the first country I considered as an overseas option, it wasn't the one we chose for the start of our overseas adventures. Julie and I chose Ecuador, where we embraced a very different and almost unbelievably affordable lifestyle.

"We enjoyed Ecuador, but, once we'd made that first move, we couldn't help but notice other options that also seemed very appealing. What could be better than Ecuador, we'd asked ourselves while enjoying our new life there, first in Cuenca, then in Vilcabamba. Then we discovered that, well, other places might just be better in some ways. So, from Ecuador, we moved to Uruguay, where we divided our time between Montevideo and Punta del Este, on the coast. What could be better than that life, split between a pleasant city and one of the world's most beautiful stretches of coastline?

"Then we discovered Brazil, where we lived right on the beach. Could we top that? In fact, we did, at least from our perspective, in Medellín. Given the quality of lifestyle and the quality of property that you're buying, this city is an extraordinary bargain.

"Then, as grandchildren appeared on the scene, our priorities shifted. We wanted to be a more regular part of our family's lives. They live in California, so we targeted Mexico. Now we're retired overseas part time, half the year in the ocean-view apartment we purchased in Mazatlan, the other six months in Sacramento."

How to Buy for Retirement

When shopping for real estate for personal use in retirement overseas, you want to think about things like:

- How much space you will need. Do you want an apartment or a house? One bedroom or two? (You probably won't need more than two.) Two levels or only one? A guest room or even a guesthouse? Will you have guests often, for example? Will you want them to be able to stay with you, or would you prefer if they came and went from a hotel nearby?
- Whether you want a front yard, a back garden, or a swimming pool. All of these things require care and maintenance.
- Location. Do you want to be in the heart of downtown or out in the country?
- Type of property. Do you like the idea of living in a gated community, or would you prefer a more integrated setting, such as a neighborhood where you could become part of the local community? This is a key consideration. Going local means you have to learn the local language (if you don't speak it already). Or perhaps you'd prefer to be off on your own with undeveloped acres between you and your nearest neighbor. In this type of rural setting, you will need to build your own in-case-of-emergency infrastructure.
- Traffic patterns and transportation. Where you base yourself determines whether you'll need to invest in a car, which is an important budget consideration.
- The convenience factor. How far is it to shopping, restaurants, nightlife, parking, and the nearest medical facility?
- Furnished versus unfurnished. You may have no choice but to buy unfurnished (unless you buy, say, from another expat who's interested in selling his place including all contents). Buying unfurnished means you'll need to purchase furniture locally or ship your household goods from home.
- Your budget. This is the most practical guideline of all, of course. Be clear on your finances before you start shopping, and, if your budget is strict, don't be tempted to consider properties outside your price point. You'll only be disappointing yourself unnecessarily.

- Finally, ask yourself what kind of view you'd like from your bedroom window each morning. This can be an effective way to focus on something important that might otherwise be overlooked until it's too late.

Are You Ready to Go Local? If Yes, You Could Retire Well on as Little as $700 per Month in These Two Places

It's possible to retire overseas and live well on as little as $700 per month. That's an extreme, though, and it's not to say that you could retire anywhere overseas on $700 per month. The choices that qualify have something else in common—they can all also be described as "local" options. By this we mean these are places where you'd be living like the locals, among the locals, shopping where the locals shop, eating where the locals eat, and speaking whatever language the locals speak. Top options for where to retire well today on a strictly limited budget include Ecuador, Nicaragua, Thailand, and Vietnam. Thailand and Vietnam are not countries we recommend for real estate investment. In both, foreign ownership of property is restricted.

The two best places right now, therefore, to consider combining the budget retiree-buyer agenda with the investor-buyer agenda are Ecuador and Nicaragua. Specifically, we'd recommend looking at Cuenca (colonial city) or Cotacachi (mountain town) in Ecuador, and Granada (oldest colonial city in the Americas) in Nicaragua. In Cuenca, you could buy a retirement residence in the center of town for as little as $850 per square meter. That's absolutely, universally cheap. It means that a 150-square-meter house or apartment (that's about 1,500 square feet), at one of the city's most central addresses, in move-in condition, can be had for as little as $125,000. In Cotacachi, you could own for less, as little as $600 per square meter. Life in Cotacachi wouldn't be for everyone. This is rural, remote Ecuador, and Ecuador is a Third-World country where you won't forget you're in a Third-World country. Still, you could own your own retirement residence here, with beautiful mountainscapes all around, for well under $100,000, and you could live in it comfortably on a budget of even $500 or $600 a month. You aren't going to match the quality of life you could enjoy in this part of Ecuador on such a minimal budget anywhere else in the world.

Nicaragua in general is slightly more expensive than Ecuador, but the costs both of living and of real estate in Granada in particular are on par with those in Cuenca. One big difference between these two retirement options is that, in Granada, you're retired at sea level (though on the shores of a lake, not the ocean), while in Cuenca, you're in the mountains. Your choice could come down to the climate you're looking for.

Best Budget Options in Europe

We'll offer two more budget-retiree choices that also present good investor-buyer opportunities. These options don't fit into the retire-on-less-than-$700-per-month category, but they are our top recommendations for where to retire on a modest budget if Third-World living isn't for you. Not everyone is cut out for life in the tropics or the developing world. If your retirement dream is more about the good life in the Old World, we suggest you look at rural France (not Provence, but west of there) or rural Italy (not Florence, but south and east of that well-known and, yes, too-expensive-for-the-retiree-on-a-budget locale). Specifically, in France's Béarn region and in Italy's Abruzzo, you could enjoy the best of country life on the Continent on a budget that qualifies as small (as little as €1,600 per month), and you would be, at the same time, combining an idyllic, Old World retirement lifestyle with an investment in a euro-denominated real asset that would provide diversification, the potential for appreciation, and a nice inheritance for your heirs. In both these regions, you could buy a home of your own for as little as €1,000 per square meter. Considered in the context of what you're buying and where, that is a very good price.

Top Tip from Lief

Meters and Measures

In nearly all the world outside the United States, real estate is measured in square meters. One square meter equals 10.76 square feet. For the purposes of rough calculations in your head, you can multiply or divide, as the case may be, by 10.

We recommend that, as you set off into the world of overseas property, you make this adjustment. Get your head around meters instead of feet and train yourself to process each piece of real estate you consider in that context. It's the best way to compare properties and prices. As there are no multiple listing services outside North America, you're going to have to make your own comparisons. The only way to do this is to use standard units of measure.

Also note that, in much of the world, land is measured not in acres but hectares. A hectare is equal to 2.47 acres. In Nicaragua, Costa Rica, and sometimes in Argentina land is measured in *manzanas*. In Nicaragua, a *manzana* is equal to 1.74 acres; in Costa Rica, it's 1.727 acres; and in Argentina, a *manzana* is a hectare. In Thailand, land is measured in *rais*; 1 *rai* is 0.395 acre. For help making these kinds of conversions, take a look at www.onlineconversion.com/area.htm.

Two Places to Live the American Retirement Dream Overseas

We've offered recommendations for where to combine the retiree's agenda with that of the investor if your retirement nest egg is small. If budget isn't a restriction for you, we'd offer two other suggestions, the two locations we believe stand out as the best places in the world to retire overseas, period.

World's Best Place to Retire Overseas: Algarve, Portugal

Monthly budget: €1,915
Monthly rent: €1,250

Algarve, Portugal, belongs at the top of the list of the world's best places to retire, thanks to its low cost of living, low cost of real estate, great weather, established expat community, user-friendly and low-cost retiree residency program, and endless options for how to meaningfully fill your days and evenings. In addition, you can get by speaking only English (thanks to the region's strong historic and cultural links with England), and, notably, the stunningly beautiful country is one of the safest places on Earth right now.

World's Other Best Place to Retire Overseas: Mazatlan, Mexico

Monthly budget: 21,940 Mexican pesos
Monthly rent: 10,000 Mexican pesos

The other best place to retire overseas today is Mazatlan, Mexico. Over the past four decades, Americans have voted Mexico the world's number-one place to live or retire in the way that really counts—they've packed up and moved there. This country is home to more American expats and retirees than any other, at least 1 million and as many as 2 million, depending on the survey.

Americans looking to start a new life in a new country primarily seek three things: warm weather, beautiful beaches, and a low cost of living. Mexico competes in all three categories. While the living is not as cheap as it was in the 1970s when Americans began migrating here in volume, it's a global bargain and more of a budgeter's delight right now than it's been in a long time, thanks to the U.S. dollar's strength against the Mexican peso.

The country is familiar, from its administrative set-up (the Mexican government is a stable democracy, with executive, legislative, and judicial branches functioning in a similar way to those in the United States) to its big-footprint shopping. If you're itching for an adventure in a foreign land that's not too foreign, Mexico could be the experience you seek. Plus, it's easy to go back and forth, making it a top choice for part-time living. Drive down as often as you like without worrying about plane fare.

Automatic six-month tourist stays and easy and fast immigration make it possible to come and go and spend as much time in the country as you'd like. You can maintain a second home here (that you rent out when you're not using it yourself) without having to bother with the expense of obtaining formal resident status.

You could return easily to the United States to use Medicare. If you're considering this move as a retiree, nearing or over the age of 65, this can be Mexico's most compelling advantage. Mexico offers excellent health care, but Medicare won't pay for it; with limited exceptions, Medicare doesn't cross any border. However, if you retire in Mexico, you'd be only a drive or quick flight away from accessing your benefits.

Among this country's many attractive lifestyle options, Mazatlan stands out. Real city, beautiful beaches, and walkable colonial center … popular expat choice and authentic Mexican resort town that manages to feel homey—Mazatlan has it all. Located about midway along Mexico's Pacific coast, Mazatlan has been out of favor among tourists and expats for decades but is making a comeback. The renaissance has been focused on the city's historic center, which has undergone an impressive face-lift and now rivals Mazatlan's 20 miles of beach for attracting attention.

3 Cash Flow from Property Overseas Can Pay for a Second Home You'd Never Be Able to Afford at Home

The reasons to buy property overseas are many but can be boiled down to simple math. In key markets across our globe, you can buy for a fraction the cost of owning something comparable in the United States.

Americans' favorite places to shop for a second home are Florida and Arizona, maybe California and the Carolinas. How much does it cost to own a two-bedroom condo on the shores of Florida or the California coast? And where else in the world could you buy that same (or even a better) condo on a comparable (or nicer) beach for less money?

Let's take a spin across the world map in search of answers to those questions. Let's compare what it costs to buy in traditional second-home and retirement locations in the States with what it'd cost you to own in a similar alternative location overseas.

Of course, no two places in the world offer exactly the same set of attractions. But we think we've found good matches—beachfront for beachfront, city appeals for city appeals, and so forth.

Texas Versus Colombia

For three years running, *U.S. News & World Report* ranked Austin, Texas, the top city lifestyle option in the United States. We name Medellín, Colombia, as the top city lifestyle option in the Americas. How does the cost of owning a second home in these two cities compare?

The average per-square-meter price for an apartment in downtown Austin is $8,025. A two-bedroom, two-bath, 117-square-meter place in a nice downtown location close to bars, restaurants, shopping, and parks, renovated to a luxury standard, with sunset views from a wraparound balcony, is listed for $599,999. That works out to $5,128 per square meter, well below the city average.

The average per-square-meter price for an apartment in central El Poblado, the best address in Medellín, is $1,456. A two-bedroom, two-bath, 115-square-meter place on El Poblado's Golden Mile, meaning minutes' walk to bars, restaurants, shopping, and parks, renovated to a luxury

45

standard, with views over the Medellín valley from the balcony, is 560 million Colombian pesos. Today that's $172,000, or $1,494 per square meter, which is slightly above the city average but 70% less than buying the same thing (*mas o menos*) in Austin. Having spent time in both cities, we'd argue that Medellín is a nicer place to be.

Florida Versus Brazil

Florida dominates Conde Nast's 10 Best Places to Retire in the United States. Its beach towns take four spots, including the top two. Top of the list is Fort Myers, offering the best of Florida's beachside lifestyle without the crowds. Sarasota takes second place and is touted as a top beach lifestyle with lower property prices than Tampa and Naples.

No compromise is required to swap Florida's sunny coast for the world-class beaches of northeastern Brazil. Fortaleza has the broadest mass appeal among Brazil's northeastern coastal cities and is a major draw for foreign residential investors. It's also a hub for Brazilians, Europeans, and North Americans seeking a second home. It's hard to beat Fortaleza's fine sandy beaches, great weather, and rich lifestyle anywhere in the world.

For better value and the opportunity for uncrowded beaches, with few to no high rises, look to the stretch of coast 90 minutes south of Fortaleza, around the popular resort town of Canoa Quebrada. That's where prices get exciting for the same great beach lifestyle.

Sarasota is a little more than an hour from Tampa, while Canoa Quebrada is 90 minutes from Fortaleza.

A two-bedroom, two-bath, 99-square-meter villa in a private community two blocks from the beach in Sarasota is $374,900. That's $3,787 per square meter.

A two-bedroom, two-bath, 100-square-meter villa just back from the beach in Canoa Quebrada is $97,000. That's $970 per square meter, 74% less than the villa in Sarasota.

South Carolina Versus Portugal

Also common on lists of the best places to live or retire in the United States is Charleston, South Carolina, known for its history, cobblestoned streets, horse-drawn carriages, and antebellum houses. It's considered one of the most charming places to call home in this country. The average per-square-meter price to own in the city center is $4,903. A 91-square-meter two-bedroom, two-bath apartment in the French Quarter near Waterfront Park is being sold for $579,900, or $6,372 per square meter.

Porto, in northwest Portugal, is likewise known for its history, cobblestoned streets, charm, and classic architecture. It's also the mouth of the Douro River, said to shimmer like liquid bullion at sunset. The average cost to own here is $2,978 per square meter. A two-bedroom, two-bath apartment 15 meters from the river is offered for $390,000, or $3,438 per square meter. That's 13% above the city average but 46% cheaper than the apartment in Charleston, and, rather than charming like the Old World, it *is* the Old World.

Top Tip from Kathleen

No One Needs to Know, Not Even the IRS

One reason real estate overseas is the smartest thing to do with your money right now has to do with privacy. As an American, no matter where you live—whether you're resident in the United States or not—you are required to report all foreign financial assets to Uncle Sam each year on what is referred to as Form 8938 if you meet the reporting criteria. There are two exceptions to the 8938 filing requirement, two foreign assets that the IRS doesn't insist on knowing about. One is gold and other precious metals held in physical form. The other is real estate if it is held in your personal name (as opposed to a foreign corporation or foreign LLC). This means that foreign real estate is one of but two remaining assets that allow an American to retain some level of privacy of ownership, not only with Uncle Sam but with potential U.S. plaintiffs or creditors, as well. How is a U.S. litigant going to seize your condo in Panama City or your beachfront lot in Belize? He's not.

4

Cash Flow from Property Overseas Can Make You Rich (While Creating Diversification, Asset Protection, and a Legacy for Your Heirs)

Property is a cornerstone of any long-term wealth strategy and building a real estate investment portfolio anywhere including in the United States can make you rich. However, we've known too many property investors who have lost everything. When this happens, it's usually a result of too much leverage and not enough diversification—investing in just one market, in the United States or overseas, or in only one type of property.

In 2005, we met a young and aggressive investor making hard-money developer loans in Iowa. He was earning 12% and scoffed when we suggested he diversify outside the United States or at least beyond Iowa. Yes, we agreed, it'd be hard to match the 12% net per year, but his portfolio and therefore his returns would be safer long term. The guy lost everything in 2008 when the bottom fell out of the Iowa market and borrowers couldn't repay his loans. We could tell you a dozen versions of that story to do with a dozen nondiversified property investors.

Over the past two-and-a-half decades, we've proven that investing in real estate overseas is a strategy for both generating reliable cash flow and building real wealth. We are confident you can make good or great money this way. We also know that slow and steady wins this race. Don't be tempted to go too big or too far too fast.

If you're starting from nothing, you'll need to build seed capital using other people's money, as Lief did in Chicago at the start of his investing career. Don't jump straight to investing in real estate overseas until you have a portfolio to diversify in the first place. That said, you don't need to be rich to invest overseas. We'll introduce you to markets where you could buy in with less than $100,000 as well as markets where you can leverage.

When we met, Lief had just sold his three-flat in Chicago, and Kathleen was preparing to sell her home in Baltimore in advance of the move to Ireland. We pooled the proceeds of those two sales to come up with the down payment for our purchase in Waterford. We sold that property for four times our investment, giving us the funds for the biggest purchase of our careers by that point in Paris.

We were able to afford Lief's preconstruction purchase on the coast of Spain, thanks to developer terms that allowed us to set aside enough each month to come up with the scheduled payments.

The cash from that flip gave us the down payment for the rental we purchased preconstruction in Panama.

A colleague has followed a similarly organic approach. He started with one preconstruction investment in Panama City, then another. Then, a few years later, he invested in Santa Marta, Colombia. Two decades from his first purchase, he holds a portfolio of rentals in Panama, Colombia, the Philippines, and Russia that earns him 20% per year. He's well diversified across economies and currencies, and he travels continuously, checking in on his holdings and scouting new markets. "Now I have my sights set on Portugal," he told us recently. "I have no European exposure, and, with the dollar strong versus the euro, it seems like the time to address that."

How do you get rich investing in real estate overseas? You make one purchase in a market generating decent yields. Rent it, setting aside the excess cash flow each month, until the property's value has appreciated to a level where it makes sense to sell. Roll over the accumulated rental income and the capital gain into a next property in a next market. Do this until you're accumulating enough excess cash flow that you can afford to buy a next investment without selling one you already own. Continue in this way, on and on, until, in time, you're a bona-fide global property baron earning enough cash flow to fund a life of travel and the retirement of your dreams.

Top Tip from Lief

Potentially Tax Deductible

Another practical benefit for an American owning real estate outside the United States has to do with your annual tax bill. The travel associated with scouting for, purchasing, and then managing a real estate investment overseas is tax deductible.

Years ago, we knew a lady named Janet who bought land on the southwestern coast of Ireland, in Kerry. On this plot Janet built two houses, one for her personal use and one to rent out. Each summer, Janet took a trip to Kerry to check on her rental property and to meet with her rental manager. During the visit, she stayed in one of the two houses she'd built, her Irish home. The income from renting out the second of the two houses covered the carrying costs and then some for both properties, with money left over to subsidize Janet's annual holidays on the Emerald Isle. Then, every April 15, Janet was able to take those travel costs as deductions on her U.S. tax return.

Start with This Key Question: How Much Can You Afford?

C an an average person really invest for cash flow overseas?

We get the question all the time. Our enthusiastically positive response isn't based on theory but on firsthand experience and observation. We've known hundreds of typical investors like you who've built globally diversified cash-flowing portfolios and who are enjoying both the income and the lifestyle that this investment strategy provides. How do you get started? How do you determine where and what to buy first?

Your lifestyle agendas and objectives should play a role in determining how you invest. More practically important is budget. How much can you afford?

You can find agricultural investments packaged for the individual investor available for as little as $30,000, and you could buy a small house or apartment that you could use part-time and rent out otherwise for $50,000 to $100,000 in a handful of proven rental markets, including Abruzzo, Italy; Béarn, France; Cuenca, Ecuador; Medellín, Colombia; Granada, Nicaragua; and Cayo, Belize.

Investing less than $100,000 in a rental property, you wouldn't be buying big or fancy, but small and modest is the way to start anyway. Big and fancy means heavy carrying costs. Property taxes usually depend on the size of the property. A big house on a big lot needs cleaning, landscaping, and caretaking. And a fancy house is one you're more likely to worry about being damaged by renters. Starting out, especially if your budget is limited, you want one or two bedrooms and standard finishes, fixtures, and furnishings. This is not to say you don't want charming. In Abruzzo and Béarn, to stick with two examples in the Old World, even $50,000 to $100,000 can buy you a lot of charm.

Finding an answer to the question "How much can you afford?" comes down to two things. First, how much capital you have available to invest? If you don't know this number already, take time right now to do the math. Second, what kind of financing or purchase terms might be available to you?

Most property markets outside the United States are cash-only. You aren't going to be able to organize local financing as a foreign (nonresident) buyer in most markets overseas. However, you do have options for leveraging whatever capital you have to invest.

5 Consider Local Financing Options (If They Exist) and How You Can Qualify

ief used other people's money (OPM) to launch his real estate investing career in the United States, and we were able to borrow for our first purchases overseas, as well.

For his first investment, in Chicago, Lief negotiated a 98% loan-to-value (LTV) loan from a local bank running a special offer, and we bought our house in Ireland with a 95% LTV financing from Bank of Ireland. While our second overseas property investment—a preconstruction condo on the coast of Spain—wasn't financed by a bank, it was made using developer terms that allowed us to pay just 5% down and then another 25% over two years, with the final 70% not due until completion of the unit.

Bank financing in the United States comes with an additional cost if your LTV is greater than 80% in the form of private mortgage insurance (PMI). Ask Lief how he got out of paying PMI for his Chicago purchase if you meet him at a conference sometime.

Private mortgage insurance isn't a requirement when borrowing to buy property in most markets overseas, but a local life insurance policy naming the lending bank as the primary beneficiary if you die before the mortgage is paid off is. You can buy the policy through the bank or from a third party, but a current life insurance policy in your home country won't qualify. More important, most life insurance companies around the world will insure you only up to age 70 or 75. That limitation restricts the mortgage term if you're older than 50 when applying for financing. A 65-year-old, for example, can qualify for a 10-year loan at best. Don't forget the cost of the life insurance when calculating your return on investment; it can take a bite out of your net yield.

Even if you're 40 or younger, don't expect a 30-year mortgage. These are uncommon outside the United States. Twenty years is typical; 25 years can be possible. Likewise, fixed-rate mortgages, with the rate fixed for the entire term of the loan, aren't typical. Expect variable-rate financing. In France, the monthly payment for our variable-rate mortgage changed only if the interest rate increased enough to extend the life of the loan more than two years beyond the original term. At one point, that happened, and our monthly payment increased.

If you're buying in a market where financing is an option for foreign buyers and you want or need a mortgage, try to get pre-approved by a bank before you begin shopping for a property to buy. This way you'll be confident of your purchase budget as well as the mortgage costs, including the monthly life insurance expense.

Local financing for nonresident foreign buyers is possible in Panama, the Dominican Republic, Portugal, France, Spain, Italy, and elsewhere in Europe. We were able to get financing in Ireland because we were resident and earning income in the country. Being able to show one or both of those things makes a big difference in your eligibility for financing; however, you aren't likely to be able to do this most places (or maybe anyplace) you want to invest.

In some markets where it's possible to borrow locally as a nonresident foreign buyer, the terms make the idea unattractive. Banks in Belize and Nicaragua, for example, offer financing to foreigners but at double-digit interest rates.

In Europe, on the other hand, interest rates are extremely low, thanks to negative central bank rates. It can be possible to qualify for a variable-rate mortgage with a starting interest rate as low as 2% or less (basically the bank's margin on lending).

Most banks around the world reference metrics similar to those used by U.S. banks when qualifying a borrower. They look at your overall debt-to-income ratio as well as the payment amount for the specific mortgage-to-income ratio. Income is more important than assets, and the easiest way to prove your income is by showing your tax return. However, if your income is from passive investments, the bank may require proof beyond your tax return—a signed statement from your tax accountant, for example. If you're self-employed, you'll have to provide additional documentation. Panama banks, which are accustomed to lending to American buyers, might also ask for a current report from a U.S. credit bureau.

In addition to asking for lots of documentation to confirm the financial information you're providing, banks overseas mitigate default risk by limiting LTV ratios for nonresident foreign buyers. The best you might typically hope for is 70%; 50% to 60% is most common, meaning you'll likely need to put down 40% to 50% when financing a property purchase overseas through a local bank.

The good news is that some banks allow you to include projected rental income as part of your personal income figures when running debt-to-expense ratios. If you're looking for a mortgage in Panama, the bad news is that banks consider credit card limit as debt even if the card has zero balance. A colleague in Panama had to pay off and close all her credit cards to qualify for a mortgage. After the mortgage had been issued, she had no problem getting new credit cards, including one from the bank that had financed her property purchase. Go figure.

Idiosyncrasies like these are why it's best to speak with a bank before you even begin your property search if you hope to use bank financing for the purchase.

However, bank financing isn't your only option ...

6 Consider Shopping for Financing Back Home or with the Developer

I f financing your real estate purchase overseas through a local bank isn't a realistic option (because the market where you want to buy doesn't lend to nonresident foreigners or because your financial situation doesn't qualify you), you have alternatives.

The first and easiest—sometimes even if local financing is available and you do qualify—can be to take out a loan back home. No, your local U.S. bank isn't going to fund your overseas real estate purchase directly. With the exception of some banks in Texas and California that have at times over the years offered loans in Mexico, U.S. banks don't have the infrastructure to protect themselves against default in a foreign country. How would they foreclose and recuperate their funds?

U.S. banks do, however, offer home equity loans and lines of credit. This was an important source of funding during the rapidly appreciating U.S. market leading up to 2008. Taking out a $100,000 equity loan, say, on your principal residence in the United States to invest in a condo at the beach in Brazil or the Dominican Republic can be a straightforward strategy. Your U.S. lending bank doesn't typically care what you use the money for as long as they're happy with the metrics to do with the value of the collateral and your debt-to-income ratio.

You should care, though. If you're lucky enough to own a piece of property in the United States that has enough equity to allow you to draw out and invest in another property in another country, make sure you run your own numbers and that you're comfortable with the math. Just because a bank will lend to you doesn't necessarily mean you should borrow.

The most important calculation to make is whether or not you can cover the payment on the equity line if your overseas rental doesn't produce the monthly income you're projecting right away. It can take time to build up a short-term rental clientele, and many short-term rental markets are seasonal, meaning inconsistent cash flows month to month even if your annual rental income should be more than enough to cover your loan payments. Run worst-case scenarios. The last thing you want is to put your primary residence or even another rental property in jeopardy.

In addition to tapping into equity you've built up back home, another option for financing over-seas can come courtesy of the developer. Developers who build for and sell to the foreign market understand that foreign buyers want and can need financing, so many offer payment programs. These can include preconstruction purchase terms, payment plans, and straight-up financing.

Developers are often happy to offer land sales with financing, because this means cash flow that can help cover the costs of installing infrastructure. Typically, with this kind of financing, you don't receive title until you've paid for the property in full. The developer is protected because he technically still owns the property. Your payments are protected by your purchase contract.

Buying preconstruction means a payment plan. This can be tied to construction milestones, or it can mean regular payments (even, for example, monthly payments made on a credit card). This isn't financing, per se, as there's no loan to value (LTV) and no interest rate and payments are due over, say, 12 to 36 months rather than amortized over 20 to 25 years. When the building is complete, you're required to come up with the final amount due, which can vary from 10% to as much as 50%.

Less common but occasionally possible is full-fledged developer financing. Typically, a developer can't afford to do this for all units in a building (because it wouldn't give him enough cash for construction), but sometimes a developer will offer this for a small number of sales. We've seen this most often in Panama and the Dominican Republic.

In some markets, you'll find sellers willing to carry back a portion of the purchase price if you're able to make a sizable down payment. Again, this is most common in markets with big pools of foreign buyers. Like developers, though, individual sellers financing a sale aren't going to give you 30 or even 20 years to pay off the loan. Three to seven years is typical. Expect to be charged interest at the going local rate. We negotiated the purchase of a building in Panama, for example, where the seller carried back the mortgage at the typical bank rate at the time but for a term of 10 years.

We'll look closely at three markets in particular, where financing is relatively easy to organize as a foreign buyer, in Part IV.

Six Strategies for Earning Cash Flow from Property Overseas

When it comes time to flip the switch to retirement, we hope to have organized our lives so that we're able to move around during that stage among a handful of destinations where we most enjoy spending time, with established infrastructure in each so that we can come and go as residents, not tourists, with friends and connections, social circles and—important to us—homes of our own.

When making your own plan for spending at least some of your retirement overseas, the starting point, key to the success of the adventure, is to be honest with yourself about what kind of lifestyle you're after. When we ask ourselves what kind of life we want in retirement, the answer is: varied. City and coastal, Caribbean and highland, spring and summer, fall and winter, developed and emerging, sophisticated and raw, refined and gritty, we appreciate it all. So we've conceived a retirement strategy, which we've been working for more than 20 years to engineer, that will allow us to enjoy it all, perpetually, in turns. We've held on to the apartment in Paris that we called home when we lived in that city with our children. This will be our co-retirement base, along with the beach house we've built on the Pacific coast of Panama, meaning we'll be able to reposition ourselves regularly between the Old World and the New. This might seem like an ambitious plan, but we've had time to evolve it.

Whatever your intentions, start developing the plan. An easy first step can be the purchase of a piece of property in a locale where you want to be able to spend time now and that you think eventually could become part of your retirement plan. Meantime, whenever you're not using the property yourself, it could be generating cash flow from rental, and, over time, it could be increasing in value, too. Your future retirement residence could be a nicely income-generating and appreciating asset on your balance sheet. Indeed, that's the ideal situation—when the holiday home-cum-retirement plan you buy also qualifies as a cash-flow investment.

That's why, when sizing up the global marketplace and the world map for potential cash-flow opportunities, a short-term rental property can be the place to start.

7 Short-term Rentals— Airbnb Is a Double-edged Sword

What's specifically important when considering a potential rental property purchase overseas? One driving consideration should be the pleasure potential for you and your family. Buy what and where you want. Balance that objective, though, against what matters most for rentals in your chosen market. This is key to maximizing cash flow. Property type and size are universally important rental factors. In most markets, a one- or two-bedroom property is more rentable than a three- or four-bedroom place. The incrementally higher rental rates you should be able to charge for a three-bedroom usually don't compensate for the higher cost of purchasing the larger apartment. While a super-high-end property might suit your personal preferences, a higher-end (read: more expensive) property probably means a lower rental return. To keep your occupancy up, you'll likely have to compete on price with the general (not high-end) market.

Here are questions to answer when considering any potential purchase of a vacation rental overseas:

- Where in your target location do people most want to stay? In Paris, for example, perhaps the world's most recession-proof rentals market, the traditionally best *arrondissements* for rental are the 5th and 6th. These are also among the priciest *arrondissements*. More affordable and also good for rental are the 4th and the 9th *arrondissements*, meaning an investment in these areas could generate better cash flow.

Take a similar approach when shopping for a rental in any city. Rather than focusing on the heart of the most rentable district, look around the fringes of the main tourist area and work your numbers to determine if the lower acquisition costs could result in a better cash flow, even with slightly lower expectations for rental price and occupancy.

When shopping for a rental in a beach location, the closer to the beach the better for occupancy. However, again, prices will be higher right at the beach so something slightly back with an ocean view might be a better buy.

- What size rentals are in demand in your target market? Again, generally speaking, one- and two-bedroom apartments are the rental sweet spot. However, a market can be overrun with rentals of this size, creating opportunities for either smaller (studios, for example) or bigger (three-bedroom) places.

In Medellín, investors are buying two- and three-bedroom apartments, even if that's more apartment than they need, because the prices are so low it's hard not to be tempted to buy bigger, and, right now, rental returns for these apartments are high. That said, a one-bedroom apartment in this city could generate the same or better cash flow. Again, it's a matter of balancing investment agenda with personal circumstances and preferences.

- Is there a high season and what's the opportunity for occupancy beyond that time? Also, when considering the rental season, remember your plan (if you have one) for personal use. Would you want to be occupying the place yourself during the season when much of your rental return otherwise might be earned?

Punta del Este, Uruguay, is a good case study in this context. The high season in this coastal resort town is mid-December through February. Over this 10-week window, you can charge outrageous rental rates. In fact, it's not uncommon to earn as much as 80% or 90% of the annual rental income during this peak-season period alone. The rest of the year, the going rental rates are a fraction of the short-term rents you can ask in January and February. That's okay, as you can earn enough during this period to make the investment worthwhile overall. Unless, of course, that's the time of year you'd want to use the place yourself. In that case, your intended rental investment could default into a holiday home for the family, period.

We've owned rental properties in more than a half-dozen countries. All of them were rented short term at one point. Some were also long-term rentals, which we'll discuss in a moment. The key to success with a rental of any kind but especially with a short-term rental is the rental manager.

Unfortunately, Airbnb, Vacation Rentals by Owner (VRBO), Booking.com, and other online marketing outlets for short-term rentals have convinced many people that they can manage their rentals themselves. That's true, in theory, and we know many people who do manage their own rental properties. However, if you decide to handle the management role yourself, your rental property is no longer an investment. It's a job. You should calculate some value for your time spent marketing, checking in guests, overseeing cleaning, maintenance, and repairs, taking inventory of the property's contents after each booking, and so on. That doesn't sound like fun to me but can work if you're living in the country where the rental is located. If you're not, we recommend against trying to self-manage. Engage local professional help.

The other problem with Airbnb is that it's made every home owner in the world believe they can make money renting out a room in their house, an apartment they inherited that they'd otherwise have sold, or their full-time residence when they go on a month's vacation. As a result, inventory in key short-term rental markets has expanded significantly. This increases competition for your rental, and it negatively impacts the marketplace. Much of this Airbnb inventory is poor quality and poorly managed, which can and does lead to lower net yields over time for all rentals in that market.

A good rental manager is going to make use of any marketing venue available. This should include Airbnb, but it shouldn't be limited to Airbnb. An experienced rental manager has a proprietary website and returning clientele. They know what clients in that market look for in a property and can give you tips on how to set up your unit for the best possible rental return. If you buy a basic property best suited for budget travelers, there's no need to spend money on things like a dishwasher, for example. However, if you invest in a high-end rental, you'll want to make sure you put in the little extras that those renters expect.

Many people are intimidated by the idea of a short-term rental because of the wear and tear on the property and because of the management hassle involved. Again, that's why you hire a rental manager. The difference between an okay rental manager and a great rental manager can be the difference between a net yield of 5% and a net yield of 8% or better. While 5% is in our acceptable range for return, an additional 3% a year adds up quickly.

The main reason to rent a property short term rather than long term in most markets is the potential for a higher net yield. It's not a given in all markets that a short-term rental will return better than one rented long term, so you should run projections. Nine times out of 10, though, short-term wins out, even after factoring in the cost of furnishings and even if the short-term market is seasonal.

The occupancy rate for our rental property in Lagos, Portugal, never broke 50% in the four years we owned it. However, the premium in short- versus long-term rates was enough to overcome the fact that, other than the weeks of Christmas and New Year's, the place didn't rent at all October through March. Had we rented that apartment on an annual lease, the gross rental income would have been about the same as our net rental income renting short term.

While short-term rentals generally generate higher gross rents, they also have greater expenses. Management fees for a short-term rental range from 15% to 35%. We've known managers who've charged more, but that's usually the case with a condo hotel type of property where, in theory, the connection to a hotel chain ensures exceptionally and consistently high occupancy rates. In theory, you still come out ahead.

You'll also have higher cleaning costs, with renters turning over every few days to every few weeks, depending on the market. Sometimes maid fees are added on top of the rent; sometimes not. You'll also likely have greater maintenance and repair bills, again thanks to all that turnover.

You need to push for a full picture of total costs to expect from the rental manager before you buy to ensure that your estimated annual net income projection is realistic.

In a seriously seasonal market like Punta del Este, a 20% occupancy rate (10 weeks over the summer) can generate a nice net rental yield. With our rental in the Algarve in Portugal, we saw occupancy in the 50% range and achieved decent yields (5% to 8% net) each year. In other less seasonal markets, you might hit 70% to 80% occupancy for a short-term rental, but don't believe a real estate agent or rental manager who promises or projects 100%. That's just not realistic. It's also not physically possible. You need to allow for turnover days.

Remember your intended market when furnishing a short-term rental but don't overspend. This is what Ikea is for. Ikea furniture looks good and doesn't cost much. We recommend the $400 sofa from Ikea over the $4,000 leather couch you like and would appreciate using when you stay in the property yourself. When the $400 sofa is damaged, so it goes. When the $4,000 couch is damaged, you've got to care.

Stick with the basics for kitchen items. Don't buy a coffee machine that requires an engineering degree to operate. Stock white dishes and simple glasses that can be replaced easily. You won't believe the rate of breakage for things like plates and coffee cups, and mismatched dishes can be a turnoff for renters. Fancy plates are less important than matching plates.

You have to expect damage with a short-term rental, and, unlike when renting long term, it'll be damage you usually won't be able to charge to a single renter. Early on in our investing career, one rental manager recommended that we cover the dining room and other wooden tables with glass. Her reasoning was simple. How much do you deduct from a security deposit for a scratch in a table? With a broken glass, you know how much it costs to buy another one, and, if you and your manager are paying attention in real time, you can bill that amount to the renter at fault. When it comes to furniture, you can't bill for damage, so you need to protect against it as best you can.

One key benefit with renting shortterm versus longterm anywhere in the world is that you can generally expect each tenant to vacate the premises at the end of their rental term. They have a plane ticket home and probably a limit on their tourist visa. The maid for our rental in Lagos complained that she'd have to shake awake hung-over 20-somethings some mornings to get them out in time for her to ready the apartment for the next renter. But, once awake, the kids grabbed their stuff and got out. It can be much more difficult and sometimes impossible legally to push long-term clients who've overstayed their lease out the door.

The more important consideration, when looking to buy to rent overseas, we would argue than what you buy is the system for managing what you buy. When you make a rental investment, you're choosing, first, a market; next, a rental manager; and, finally, a property. Specifically, what expertise are you looking for in a rental manager? The best ones we've hired have impressed us with their discriminating judgment. One, in Paris, made a point of telling us, with a voice of long experience, to whom she would not rent—"We won't rent to such-and-such people, because they throw wild parties" … "We won't rent to so-and-so people, because they don't respect other peoples' property" … and so forth. In some contexts, her positions might be considered discriminatory and politically incorrect. We saw them as risk management, and managing risk is a critical part of being a long-distance landlord. There are so many ways things can go wrong. You need systems to manage bookings, renter comings and goings, payments, expenses, cleaning, inventory, repairs, maintenance, renter complaints, keys, and breakage. Plus, you need a system for generating reservations. Where will you advertise? How will you market? That's perhaps the most important thing a good management company brings to the table—a developed marketing and reservations system. In addition, a good management company should:

- Be flexible enough to accommodate reservation changes and to fill the gaps. Say you've got someone in your place for two weeks; then, after Renter #1 departs, three days later someone arrives for another two-week stay. A good management agency (in an active market) will fill a couple of those gap nights.
- Meet and greet every renter. A representative from the management company should meet each renter, deliver the keys, explain systems (how the DVD player works … the trick to using the dishwasher … where to find the air-conditioning controls), suggest restaurants and services in the area, answer questions, and so forth. Some of these things should also be explained in full in a Renter's Manual, conspicuously displayed in the property.
- Perform a postrenter check to look for damages, to verify inventory, and to confirm cleaning.
- Keep a detailed and current inventory of everything in the unit from wine glasses to pillowcases.
- Contact you immediately if he notices anything damaged or broken.
- Solicit estimates for necessary repairs, oversee the repairs, and update you in real-time about the associated costs.
- Send you (by e-mail) regular reports (say, monthly) on occupancy, nightly rental rates, expenses, fees, taxes, and (with luck) profits.
- Respond to your e-mails. You'd be surprised how many times this final point becomes the most challenging.

One agency we worked with in Paris regularly left renters standing alone and confused outside the front door to the apartment building awaiting someone to show up with the key to let them inside. Another agency we worked with in Paris never thought to keep an inventory of the apartment contents. We'd visit to check on things to discover that there was a single drinking glass in the cabinet or but two lonely forks in the cutlery drawer.

It's the exceptional agency anywhere that remembers to factor in all related expenses, fees, taxes, and so on, in projections and, even, in reporting. In Paris, for example, don't forget the building fee (it's called the *syndic* fee) or the local property taxes that you, the owner, are liable for (called the *taxe d'habitation* and the *taxe fonciere*). And don't forget to plan for the things that can't be planned for—leaks in the bedroom ceiling, exploding water heaters, lost keys (it costs $150+ per to have a key made in France), and so forth.

How do you find a good rental manager? Ask for references from other landlords who've been invested in the market for some time. Interview at least two. Go with a professional. By this, we mean someone who is focused full-time and working to make money. We've made the mistake of engaging folks who managed apartment rentals on the side, as a hobby, or as a part-time occupation in retirement. We wouldn't make that mistake again. You want someone with an established infrastructure (for advertising, taking reservations if you're renting short-term, negotiating contracts if you're renting long-term, reporting, etc.); existing support (for meeting tenants upon arrival with the keys, responding to tenants' cries for help turning up the heat in the middle of the night, and managing things like inventory in the case of a furnished rental); and a proven track record (for bringing in renters, keeping track of cash flow, and making sure the local tax and utility bills are paid on time). You don't want to work with the friend of a friend who has been managing his own apartment rental for a couple of years and who is now looking to expand to manage others' investments, as well.

In most markets, things like commission structure and percentage and what's included for that fee are standardized, though you want to confirm and clarify this in every case.

Top Tip from Kathleen

Note that property management and rental management can be two different things. Some rental managers are also willing and able to act as property managers but charge an additional fee.

Your rental manager is responsible for keeping your rental rented. You're paying them for their marketing infrastructure and their ability to bring you tenants. Your property manager is responsible for managing and maintaining the rental property itself. You're paying this person to take care of cleaning, to manage repairs, to keep a property contents inventory, to replace supplies and broken/damaged items, and to pay local bills and expenses (the electric, phone, and annual tax bills, etc.).

Rental management is usually billed as a percentage of gross rental income. Property management is typically a flat monthly fee. The combined costs of property and rental management range from 20% to 40% of rental income, depending on the market.

8

Long-term Rentals— Here's the Single Secret to Success and Maximum Return

A few years ago, on a visit to Paris to check on one of our rental apartments there, we sat down one afternoon with our rental manager, Linda.

"Every one of my apartments is rented," she told us. "In fact, I need more inventory."

Yet, at the time, our apartment had been vacant since our tenant of one year had vacated a few months earlier. Three months without cash flow later, we were growing concerned.

"If all of your apartments are rented, and you could fill more if you had them," we couldn't help but wonder aloud with Linda that afternoon, "why is ours sitting vacant?"

"But you said you wanted long-term rentals only," Linda replied. "We will find one, I'm certain. It will just take more time."

"But if we allowed short-term renters?" we asked.

"Oh, I'd have someone in here within two weeks. If you were open to short-term clients, you could have been fully occupied these past three months, just like all my other apartments."

One of the advantages of real estate investing overseas in general and of rental investments overseas in particular is that, when an asset isn't returning according to expectations, you can adjust the asset. Did you buy a house in a resort region where there's a lot of competition for rentals? Improve your chances of attracting would-be renters' attention by adding a swimming pool. Did you invest in an apartment in a place without zoning restrictions and you're having trouble finding tenants? Try advertising your asset as commercial rather than residential. Are you struggling to fill your long-term rental in Paris? Offer it on the short-term market.

There are arguments to be made both for and against renting long versus short term. For us, the biggest short-term minus is the wear and tear it can mean on the property. Holidaymakers coming and going week after week take less care and cause more damage than a retired couple settled in for a couple of years. Each new renter must learn how to use the dishwasher, the washing machine, and the heating system. In the process, breakage is unavoidable. A tourist staying in an apartment for a week or two isn't going to replace a glass or a dish when he breaks one, but someone living in the place for a year eventually has no choice. With short-term tenants, keys get lost, and knick-knacks disappear. You accept all this as a cost of the investment.

Long term comes with a downside, too. If your place is rented 100% of the time, you can never use it yourself. In addition, in most markets, long term typically means reduced net return.

However, the biggest downside to renting long term in another country is that, unlike the short-term vacation renter who can be counted on to return home, long-term renters have rights. These rights vary country by country, but without exception they favor the tenant over the landlord. That's why, in many markets, it's almost impossible to find an unfurnished long-term rental. It's easier to evict a tenant if they don't have to move the furniture out with them.

We first learned that secret when we moved to Ireland and needed to find a place to rent while we shopped for a home to purchase. We were happy that every rental we looked at was being offered furnished. The furniture we'd shipped from the United States was on a boat somewhere in the Atlantic Ocean. It wasn't until we had moved into our house and started looking at investing in a rental property that we discovered furnished was the only option for purchase. When we asked why, we were told about the country's tenant laws.

Friends who moved to France wanted to rent an unfurnished apartment so they could buy furniture they found comfortable rather than making do with furniture the landlord found convenient and affordable. They discovered that the terms for a long-term unfurnished rental were much harsher than those for a long-term furnished apartment. To rent unfurnished, they would have had to have "sequestered" two years of rent in their bank account. That amounted to freezing a not insignificant amount of money. It was still in their account, but they couldn't access it until they moved out of the apartment. What if, they wondered, they lived in the place for 10 years? That's a long time not to have access to tens of thousands of euros, which could be released only by a letter from the landlord.

Why two years of rent? Because that's how long it can take to evict someone in France.

Rule number 1, therefore, if you want to rent long term, is to furnish your property. Rule number 2 is not to rent to citizens of the country where the property is located. This isn't racist but practical. People from the place where you're investing are likely to know much more about tenant rights and what they can get away with than a foreigner would.

We've successfully rented one of our furnished apartments in France long term. Our tenants ranged from a Japanese bank manager on a one-year temporary assignment to a law professor on sabbatical with his wife. As an aside, the law professor was a pain in the neck, despite not being French, which led to a third rule to do with long-term rentals: No lawyers.

You can charge a premium for a furnished long-term rental compared with an unfurnished property. However, it's not much of a premium so, remember, Ikea is your friend.

It's easier to manage a long-term rental than a property being rented short term. Still, we recommend hiring a local to help. You need someone on the ground to make sure the rent is paid and to be your representative for any tenant problems. The rental agent fee for long-term rentals around the world is generally the same as in the United States—one month's rent, or 8.33% of the annual rent. In some markets, a flat 10% of the annual rent is normal. If you're renting long term but for less than a year, say a six-month lease, the fee could be as high as 15% of the total rent during the lease period. In some markets, including France, the renter pays the rental management fee.

You may also need to engage a property manager to help with a rental overseas. If you're not in the country to deal with repairs or other tenant issues and to pay the bills, you need help. The property manager can be the same person or agency as the rental manager or it could be handled separately. Property management is typically a flat fee, say between $50 and $150 per month.

If you decide to take the risk and rent your place long term but unfurnished, make the security deposit amount big enough to protect your interest (like the French do). This might be unusual in some markets and some potential tenants will object, but better to reduce your pool of renters than to make yourself vulnerable in this way.

Top Tip from Lief

Even if you're renting furnished, you may want to charge more than one month's rent for the security deposit. In Panama, for example, it's not uncommon for long-term tenants to move out before the end of their lease without paying the final month's rent. They leave figuring their security deposit covers them. However, it doesn't cover you if they leave your property damaged.

Your Rental Investment Will Not Be Successful without These Three Things

Your return from any rental investment overseas depends first and foremost on the market. Are there renters enough to go around? Consider both the supply of rentals and the existing or anticipated demand. You may need to break things down, as different rental markets may exist in parallel—one for tourists and another for executives on extended-stay contracts, for example. A family of holidaymakers is looking for a different kind of rental property than a banker from Japan on assignment, even if each is shopping for a rental in the same area of the same city.

The second key to a good rental return, as we've discussed, is the rental manager. A good manager can translate to a good return from a decent rental in a decent market. A bad manager can mean no return, even from a great rental in a booming market.

The third variable affecting return is the type of rental you choose to buy and what you do with it. In most markets, a one-bedroom makes most sense, but there are exceptions. In Paris, for example, one-bedroom rentals are a glut on the market. Two-bedroom rentals are in shorter supply, meaning that, if you can afford it, a two-bedroom can make more sense and yield greater return.

In a beach market, a beachfront unit is key. People are coming for the sand and the sea. Front-line units will always enjoy better occupancy. In a city high-rise market, you want a building with an elevator, a doorman, security, competitive building amenities (in Panama City, for example, lots of new inventory is coming online and renters are choosing based on building amenities as much as any other factor; the newest buildings have the best amenities), parking, and day-to-day services (grocery store, newsstand, restaurants, dry cleaners, etc.) within walking distance.

A property that works for short-term rental generally works for long-term rental as well, but the reverse is not always true. When shopping for a property you intend to rent long term, therefore, it's smart to focus in areas that would work for a short-term market, too. That way you could switch from one type of rental to another should your situation or the market change. Flexibility is a good thing.

You're Also Buying the Building

Lief was recently elected to the board of directors for the owners' association of a building in Panama City where we own a rental property. The experience is giving us insights into what goes into maintaining a 27-story building. Every owner has his pet peeves and grievances. Lief and his fellow board members listen to them all, meantime spending hours each week trying to keep the building functioning, maintained, and constantly improving.

This speaks to another thing to remember when shopping for a rental investment unit anywhere in the world—in addition to the apartment, you're also buying the building where it's located.

We know of a building in Panama City that has no working elevator. A recent advertisement for an apartment for sale on the 14th floor of this building tried to make the best of the situation. It read: "No need for a gym membership when you live here." The price was attractive and reflected the lack of elevator access. The problem is that, eventually, the broken elevator will have to be replaced. This will trigger a special assessment on all building owners. This isn't uncommon. If the cash flow from regular monthly building fees isn't enough to cover both the costs of operating the building and of required maintenance and necessary improvements, well, the money has to come from somewhere.

Or not. And this is the risk. If owners aren't organized and working together, the building and your investment suffer. It won't be possible to get the consensus needed to execute special capital calls, to increase the amount of the monthly building fees, or to carry out big-ticket repairs or improvements. The bottom-line result is that the public areas and amenities in the building will deteriorate.

When trying to identify a rental investment, therefore, shop not only location, unit, and price per square meter, but also building and building management. Ask about the building association and ask to see the related documents, including minutes from recent association meetings, financial statements for the building fund, and details of building improvements planned or being considered. Years ago, shopping for our first rental apartment investment in Paris, a friend made a recommendation that we probably didn't appreciate enough at the time. "Try to find out if any big improvements are planned for the building within the next year or two," he told me. "Are they going to add an elevator? Clean the building façade? Relay the cobblestones in the courtyard? Fix a leaking roof?"

Why? Because these are extraordinary expenses that will have to be paid for by a capital call on all owners. To avoid surprises in your first years as an owner, try to find out what kinds of works are being discussed. In France, the *syndic*, or building management association, is a legal entity with a lot of teeth. If your *syndic* tells you that you have to pony up an additional 2,000, 5,000, or even 10,000 euros in a year to cover repairs or improvements to the building, you have no choice but to comply. Well, you can choose not to comply, but the consequences are severe.

In Panama, on the other hand, building associations are haphazard and mismanaged. Sometimes they exist in name only. If the owners don't pay their monthly building fees, what are the building managers and other apartment owners going to do? In any given building in Panama City, you have a percentage, sometimes significant, of absentee owners, foreigners who bought the unit as a speculation or a rental investment. They're in the States, Canada, Germany, Venezuela, or wherever. How is the typical ad-hoc and mismanaged management team in Panama going to chase them down for their $200 a month? The effects of this are beginning to become evident in some buildings in Panama's capital. Broken elevators, faulty plumbing, ill-maintained swimming pools, unkempt social areas, and so forth.

What's your rental apartment worth when the building where it's located is falling down around it? What's your rental return going to be long term?

How to Project Rental Cash Flow

As we've suggested, your target return should be 5% to 8% net per year over the long term. However, projecting your true net return can be complicated, because the expenses of owning, maintaining, and renting vary market by market and property type by property type and change over time. This is why many in the business of trying to sell you on a particular rental investment opportunity prefer to speak in terms of gross yields. Don't let them. Drill down to a net figure.

The rule of thumb for long-term rentals in the United States is 1% of the property value per month, or 12% gross return per year. However, the net on that gross could be less than 5%, depending on your costs. Depending on the state where you're operating, for example, property taxes can take a big bite out of your gross cash flow. By way of comparison, the gross return from a rental we own in Panama City right now is 9%. Our net in this case is more than 8%, thanks to low costs and low property taxes.

Another point when projecting and tracking your yields: Understand the difference between making your calculations on original purchase price versus current value. Rental yields work like bond yields. If the property value goes down and the cash flow remains the same, then the yield goes up. And vice versa. Calculating current yields on the purchase price of a piece of property can lead to bad decisions, especially if you've owned the property for a long time or prices have recently spiked.

Returning to our Panama City rental example, the net yield based on purchase price would be more than 13%, because we bought the apartment years ago when prices were lower than they are today. That return, though, is misleading. If we sold the property and reinvested the proceeds in another investment, we wouldn't be able to realize the same yield on the greater capital amount.

A colleague in Bali got our attention a few years ago by quoting rental yields of up to 18% per year in that market; however, when pushed for details, it turned out that true net yields were running more in the range of 5% to 6%. That is, they were typical. References to exceptionally high yields are one of two things—blatantly untrue (once you drill down to true net) or the result of a market distortion creating a window of opportunity that won't last long. A few years ago, for example, you could, in fact, earn double-digit net yields from a beach rental in Punta del Este. After a couple of years, though, the gap between cost of acquisition and annual rental revenues narrowed, and, today, net yields on this part of Uruguay's coast are in the range of what you should more or less expect generally, anywhere in the world—5% to 8%.

9

Hard Money Loans—Earn Double-digit Returns Helping Other Investors

A rental can have a place in every property investor's portfolio, but it's only one way to generate cash flow from real estate overseas. Another less-common strategy that you may never have heard of is referred to as a hard money loan. We're not talking about becoming a loan shark, but you can earn double-digit returns lending money to a property developer or even a fellow investor overseas. These hard money loan opportunities come in various forms. The typical borrower is a developer looking to fast-track a project, an individual looking for financing for a property purchase in a market where it isn't available otherwise, or a company funding individual renovation projects.

This kind of one-to-one lending takes place in the United States, too, where people borrow to buy a run-down property, fix it up, and flip it. Maybe they have the capital or bank financing available for the property purchase but need cash to cover the renovation costs. An individual or an organized private group lends to the renovator at an interest rate much higher than the going rate for a bank mortgage. The borrower accepts the terms because he doesn't intend on accruing interest long. The plan is to flip the property and pay off all debt as soon as possible after the renovation has been completed.

The borrower is able to fund his or her project quicker and more easily than if they had to battle bank bureaucracy, and the property serves as collateral for the lender, either a first or a second mortgage. Developers overseas find it easier to skip bank bureaucracy, as well.

One personal experience with a hard money loan was with a developer in Australia. The interest rate was 12%, the term 18 months. The collateral was the land for development.

The developer was the sort we like—what we refer to as a serial developer. He had years of experience with relatively small and quick projects, meaning he could show a track record of getting in and out, from land purchase to sale of the completed units, in less than three years, again and again. He could have borrowed for his next project from a bank, but bank approval, even if you qualify easily for the loan, can take months. Instead, he opted to approach a broker and was able to raise the money he needed in a matter of weeks. We were fortunate enough to be communicating with the broker at the time the developer made contact.

A larger developer needing money for construction might seek a hard money loan to avoid being at the mercy of a bank's schedule for release of funds. Local housing developers in Latin America are increasingly choosing to take this route. They seek individual investors to fund the construction costs of a specific house. Eliminating bank loan paperwork and bank construction draw schedules allows the developer to move more quickly. The investor gets the lot and the house under construction as collateral.

Top Tip from Lief

A hard money loan is a riskier proposition than buying a rental property. Accordingly, the rewards can (and should) be higher. You should expect to earn interest at a rate of 10% to 16% or more. Also, this is a short-term proposition, making it a good complement to a rental property. Typically, you'll be repaid your investment capital and interest in 24 months or less.

A big part of the risk is that you're not in control of the asset. You are at the mercy of the developer, relying on his ability to complete the construction and sell the end unit. The further along a project is in the development cycle, the less risky the proposition. Make sure the developer already has all permits and construction contracts in place and confirm his marketing plan for selling the end units. One local housing developer we've worked with for a hard money loan in Panama came to us with a list of buyers looking for housing and pre-approved for bank financing. On the strength of that built-in buying pool, we moved ahead.

You could also lend directly to a property buyer. This is a less turn-key approach. You'll need to engage an attorney to make sure that a mortgage is properly filed in your favor. However, in this case, when lending to an individual directly, you can set the terms. You just need to find a borrower who'll agree to them. A three- to seven-year loan is typical. Payments can be interest only, based on a 30-year amortization with a balloon payment, or anything else you'd like to propose. You can also set the currency for the loan—either dollars or the local currency.

To find borrowers, speak with real estate agents in the market where you're interested in investing. Investors typically ask agents if they have properties on their books from sellers willing to carry a mortgage. Those buyers could be potential borrowers for you.

You can also ask the real estate attorney you're working with if he has any clients looking for financing for the purchase of property. In many markets where financing is not available to foreigners, you'll find property buyers open to a private loan even at higher than typical interest rates. They understand that leverage enhances returns.

In Colombia, one attorney we work with received so many inquiries about property financing that his firm put together a program to match buyers with people looking to lend. The program started small, with foreign investors funding foreign property investors. Over time it grew to include foreigners wanting to buy personal residences and eventually local buyers who didn't want to deal with local bank financing.

The cash flow to the investors lending money was impressive. The program made it possible to earn double-digit returns backed by real estate in Medellín and to do it in a turnkey way, without any of the hassle of being a landlord.

10 Preconstruction—Buy Before the Property Is Built to Leverage and Flip and Multiply Your Return

Buying preconstruction, or off-plan, as it's referred to in the UK and Ireland, isn't necessarily a cash-flow investment, but it can be if you keep the property and rent it out. Many investors, though, see a preconstruction purchase primarily as an opportunity for leverage. You take control of the asset by paying just a portion of the purchase price—typically 20% to 50%—over the construction period. And you buy for a discounted price.

We've made preconstruction purchases pursuing both strategies. We bought a preconstruction condo in Spain with the intent to flip it before taking possession, and we purchased preconstruction in Panama intending to keep the asset for rental indefinitely. Both of these experiences rank among our top 10 investments in terms of profitability. The apartment in Panama, which we still own, has come with a lifestyle bonus.

The condo in Spain was, in fact, our first pure real estate investment play overseas. Lief took a research trip along the southern coast of Spain, driving from Barcelona to Huelva, stopping in each active real estate market along the way. In the Costa del Sol, he came across a developer who had just released a beachfront project the day before. Forty percent of the apartments had already been reserved.

Having already seen hundreds of properties on the trip, Lief was convinced that this project was the opportunity he'd come looking for. It had all the characteristics of a successful preconstruction investment. The location was at the edge of the then Costa del Sol hot zone. The timing was perfect, as the developer had just released the first building of a multibuilding complex. Even with 40% of the units sold, several prime units remained available. The terms were standard for the time and the market, requiring ongoing construction payments totaling 30% of the purchase price. That worked for our budget. Foreigners could get financing in Spain at the time for 70% loan-to-value (LTV), meaning we could borrow the balance due when the apartment was completed in 24 months.

In addition, the developer was willing to relist investor units for sale. As our plan was to flip the property before closing on the contract and having to make the final 70% payment, that sealed the deal for us.

We signed the purchase agreement, then immediately asked the developer to list the apartment for sale. We made the construction payments over the next 18 months, as they came due, and we began speaking with banks about a loan to pay the 70% we'd be liable for at closing if it came to that. Then, four months before our unit was scheduled to be completed, meaning we'd be required to close, the developer notified us that he had a buyer. We resold the apartment a few weeks later. The buyer sent us our 30% deposit and our profit after the 5% commission fee to the developer. He paid the 70% balance when the apartment was ready. In 22 months, we almost doubled the 30% we had put down for the purchase. The annualized return worked out to 38%. Now if only we could repeat that every 22 months.

This investment was textbook. It played out exactly how every investor who has ever bought preconstruction with the intention of flipping before taking possession has hoped the experience would go. One important reason for this was that the market remained robust throughout the construction period. One risk to buying preconstruction in a market like Costa del Sol at the time, where new buildings are going up everywhere, is excessive inventory, meaning continually expanding competition for your unit when you list it for sale.

Another reason this apartment sold easily before completion was that the building was beach-front. You walked out the patio door of the apartment and across the common area of the complex directly onto the sand. Most preconstruction projects Lief saw on that research trip were back from the beach. They were either large cookie-cutter complexes with no charm or golf course projects. Being on a golf course can be a plus, but being right on the beach in a resort market is a guaranteed advantage when it comes time to resell.

Had the apartment not sold, we would have financed the rest of the purchase price and rented the property on the short-term market. We'd have kept it listed for sale, however, because we wanted the capital that was tied up in the unit for next investments.

Another preconstruction purchase, made in Panama City, Panama, in 2003, was bought with the intent of holding on to the apartment indefinitely and renting it short term. The Panamanian developer had designed a building specifically to attract foreigner investors. It would be built in the heart of the city, overlooking the Bay of Panama, and it would contain one-bedroom apartments only. This was uncommon. Historically, apartments in this high-rent district of Panama City were three and four bedrooms, which suited high-end Panamanian buyers. However, in the early 2000s, Panama began attracting growing numbers of foreign tourists and retirees, demographics in the market for smaller apartments in prime locations. This building was the first of that kind.

The terms were better than in Spain. We paid only 20% during construction and 80% at completion. Banks in Panama were lending 80% to nonresidents, and we were able to put financing in place long before the building was finished. The construction period had been projected at 30 months but extended to 40. That deferred our cash flow; however, as soon as the building was completed, we furnished the apartment for short-term rental (this was before the 45-day short-term rental restriction in Panama City discussed in Part III, Chapter 9), and we were in the

Panama City cash-flow business. Hotels were expensive in this city at the time, and tourism was expanding faster than anyone had anticipated. New hotels were planned, but, until they came online, we Panama City short-term landlords enjoyed a window of extraordinary return. During the 18 months we rented that apartment on a short-term basis, we achieved an annualized net yield of 16%.

Hotel inventory expanded, hotel developers lobbied the government to restrict short-term rental inventory, and the market slowed. Meantime, the demand for furnished long-term rentals had increased, as the dozens of international businesses setting up operations in Panama City were bringing in thousands of foreign executives and managers, all of whom wanted international-standard apartments in good locations. Ours qualified, so we stopped offering it short-tern and began marketing it as a furnished long-term rental. Another example of the upside of buying a property that works for as many different potential renter pools as possible.

While we had always planned to hold on to our unit, many other preconstruction buyers flipped. The value of their investments increased over the construction period. Some made as much as 100% on their 20% down payments over about four years. That's not 38% annualized, but it's nothing to sneeze at.

Top Tip from Lief

After the 2008 global real estate collapse, some preconstruction developers began adding clauses in their contracts specifically disallowing a buyer to resell his unit before the building had been completed. Even before 2008, U.S. developers making preconstruction offers were limiting the number of units a single investor could buy. Check the terms of the contract before you sign to make sure they don't conflict with your investment goals.

11 Agriculture—Buy Land to Rent to a Farmer

Would you rather own ALL the gold in the world or ALL the farmland?

—*Warren Buffett*

Post the 2008 crisis, property prices fell around the world, dramatically in some cases. Still, rental yields in many markets worked out to less than our 5% to 8% threshold, even when figured against post-bubble property values. Worthwhile cash-flow rental opportunities, which, until the global property boom reached its peak, had been our primary investment focus, were hard to find.

In 2009, we turned our attention to agriculture. We've always been fans of land and trees. Until this point, though, we hadn't identified a way to earn turnkey cash flow from them.

Agricultural land on which to grow cash crops, fruit trees, grape vines, or timber will always hold value, because the world is always going to need those things. Population growth (the human race is expected to increase by 2 billion people to reach nearly 10 billion by 2050) and limited and shrinking amounts of arable land (the earth has lost a third of its arable land due to erosion and pollution in the past 50 years) are combining to create a global food crisis that is going to grow more severe in coming years and decades, making productive land the ultimate hard asset.

By definition, productive land is an opportunity to produce something of marketable value, meaning, unlike a lot in a development community or a plot in the middle of a commercial district, productive land always retains the potential for yield. When whatever you plant or herd reaches maturity, you have a highly in-demand product to sell.

Many in today's investment world are talking about farmland as the new asset class. It isn't. It's the world's oldest asset class. The old real estate investment adage recommends buying beachfront because they're not making anymore of it. The limited supply and fast-growing demand make farmland at least as strong a store of value long term.

The trouble is we're not all interested in becoming farmers. That's okay because, although this can be about farming, you do not have to be willing to roll up your sleeves and pick up a hoe to earn cash flow from crops. Over the past decade-plus that we've been focused on this cash-flow strategy, we have identified three ways to play it for as much as double-digit return over decades and even generations.

Top Tip from Lief

When making any agriculture investment, you're buying for the cash flow. These can be the most profitable investments in your total portfolio.

A soy operation we know in Uruguay is returning high single digits, and we know many fruit tree and hydroponic opportunities projecting annualized returns of as much as 30%. A hydroponics investment should yield an annualized return in the range of 15% to 19%, while timber should return at least 10% to 15% annualized.

When comparing one investment opportunity with another, take into account the non–cash-flow years. You can have to wait four or five years for cash flow from an investment in a fruit tree plantation, whereas an investment in hydroponics-grown lettuce should begin generating return in 18 months.

Uruguay—The World's Best Place to Earn Cash Flow from Farmland

Looking at a world map, three places are most interesting in this context: Africa, Eastern Europe, and South America. Among the three regions, South America is the most competitive; Africa and Eastern Europe are more volatile, with more corruption, lack of clear rules, and restrictions on foreign ownership. In South America, Uruguay, in particular, stands out; about 95% of the land in this country is farmable. Until the start of this century, most of Uruguay's land was used for cattle. When farmers began to recognize the implications of the coming global population crisis, they switched from cows to soybeans (and other crops). Because Uruguayans haven't farmed their land for 200 years, it's virgin. There's been no soil degradation, as in more recognized global breadbaskets.

Foreign and local investors are treated the same in Uruguay; there are no restrictions on foreign ownership or use of land. No exchange controls or currency restrictions either. Uruguay is a foreigner-friendly, investor-friendly place and, as a result, has enjoyed the highest rate of foreign direct investment per capita of all Latin America for the past three years.

Uruguay sees even rainfall year-round, plus the country sits on the world's largest untapped aquifer. The climate is temperate, with four mild seasons. Farmers can raise two crops per year.

Uruguay's farmland market is transparent. The entire country has been surveyed for productivity levels. Each land parcel has an ID number. You can plug this number into a map (available online: www.prenader.gub.uy/coneat) to see the productivity rating for whatever piece of land interests you. The system amounts to a multiple listing service (MLS) for farmland quality, making it uncommonly easy to compare all your options at once. The average productivity rating for the country is 100. A lower rating means you're looking at land that's really suitable for running cattle only. You want land rated 120 or 130 or better. Price correlates to productivity rating.

What could you produce? Almost anything you could imagine, from cash crops (soybeans, wheat, rice, etc.) to cattle or sheep for dairy, forestry (eucalyptus, pine), vineyards, olives, blueberries ... None of these is a new crop to Uruguay. If you're buying for investment, plant soybeans (to sell to China). If you're buying for investment and fun, try a hobby crop, like blueberries or grapes.

You could buy 50 acres to thousands of acres. One of the many unique things about farmland investing in this country is that there are brokers with access to available farm investment opportunities across the country. All things considered, farmland in Uruguay is one of the most turnkey, user-friendly property purchases you could make anywhere in the world.

What would you do with your land once you'd bought it? You could either rent it out or hire a farm manager. A farm manager is like a property manager for a rental property. He is the key to your success. In Uruguay, farm management is a sophisticated industry, meaning your options can be turnkey. Leasing out your land rather than hiring a farm manager means a lesser but more reliable return, of about 4% a year. Many people buy and rent out for a year, then, when they're more comfortable with the idea, hire a farm management company for the greater yield.

Farmland in Uruguay can be both an investment and a lifestyle, even a retirement plan. You could buy a small working farm (say 10 to 15 acres) with a small house (say 1,500 square feet) for $300,000 to $400,000. Engage a farm management company to maximize the return from whatever crop you decide to farm while keeping perhaps some small field for your own use.

The two biggest objections to the idea of investing in farmland for cash flow are the hassle of managing a farm and the capital investment required to achieve reasonable economies of scale. The farming concern can be overcome by hiring a management company or renting out the land to an actual farmer, as you can easily do in Uruguay, for example. However, the investment amount necessary to achieve a worthwhile return can be seriously restrictive. To make the math work, you need to be prepared to put up at least $500,000 to $1 million. Otherwise, unless you do much of the work yourself, the costs and administration eat up the yield. If you want to become a farmer, fair enough. However, then you're talking about a job and a business, not a passive cash-flow investment.

Annual Cash Crops for Turnkey Farming Cash Flow

One way to invest in agriculture, short of buying your own million-dollar farm, is through shares of a company. This approach can take different forms.

A group we know in Argentina offers units in an investment company that rents arable land and engages a manager to farm it. The difference between the rent and the cost of the manager equals the profits distributed to the shareholders. This approach is highly leveraged (because the company doesn't own anything), meaning the risks are high relative to the potential return. On the other hand, it's an option that requires a nominal investment amount.

We prefer a different model, one that allows the investor to hold title to the land being farmed and then contract with an in-place farm management company to take care of operations. It's a miniaturized version of buying a million-dollar farm and hiring a farm manager. The farm manager cares for multiple individual properties. Each owner receives the revenue from the production from his or her property. If something goes wrong with the farm management, you still own the land.

Unfortunately, this model doesn't work everywhere because segregating and titling farmland into plot sizes small enough to make the investment affordable for the typical individual investor are restricted or disallowed by local law in many countries (making this a critical detail to confirm before investing, as we discuss in more detail in Part VII). In some markets, where the segregation is possible, it's expensive, meaning that, even if a developer is legally able to title his land in marketable chunks, the cost can be prohibitive.

This is often the case in Europe, where project developers, therefore, sometimes sell a contract allowing the right to the land and its production. The specifics vary, but, essentially, the investor owns the plants, the trees, or the vines and their resulting harvests. Usually it's trees. We know opportunities in Spain and France, for example, that allow you to buy, say, 100 trees. The farm management company takes care of your trees along with those of hundreds or thousands of other investors. They harvest the production, and you get your share of the revenue after farm management costs have been taken off the top.

Owning trees or vines isn't as secure as owning the land they're growing on, making this less a real estate play than a straightforward cash-flow investment, but the level of cash flow can make the increased risk worthwhile.

The cost of farm management depends on the investment strategy but comes in two parts.

In some cases, including when you're investing in trees, plants, or vines, you'll pay an annual crop care fee. Assessing specific direct costs for one plot of land versus another can be difficult, so the farm manager charges a flat fee per unit of land. Because you won't have revenue from a farm investment for several years (you have to wait for the trees to be planted and then to begin producing), many developers include the first X number of years of farm management in the purchase price. After that, the crop-care fee is deducted from the revenue generated.

If you're investing in a plantation growing an annual crop, direct costs are easier to account for. These types of projects typically charge variable annual costs for planting and maintenance, depending on the crop.

In addition, you'll pay the farm manager a fee related to the harvesting and marketing of the crop production. This is usually calculated as a percentage of the revenue from the crop. We like this approach, because it aligns the farm manager's interests with your own. You can figure 15% to 40% for this, depending on the type of produce.

One more related cash flow from agriculture opportunity we like is another step away from titled land. We're speaking of an investment in a hydroponic farm. As the global food crisis worsens, this type of food production, which requires no land, is going to become increasingly popular and common. As an investor, you own the production system. Farm management is handled as it is for a dirt-based farm. The farm manager plants the seeds in your system, maintains the plants, harvests the crop, sells the production, and pays you your share of the proceeds.

No matter the production or ownership method, the small individual investor (like you and us) benefits in every case from the economies of scale. We don't have to support the total investment in roads, water and irrigation systems, electricity, fencing, or any other plantation infrastructure. And we don't have to manage farm workers or get our own hands dirty.

Top Tip from Kathleen

When shopping turnkey agriculture investment options, in addition to the cost of the investment and the projected yield, consider the timeline to your first cash flow. Potential harvests include annual field crops (including soy beans, for example); tree fruits, berries, nuts; and lettuce, herb, and tomato hydroponic systems; each with its own harvest and payout schedule.

Most fruit trees are grafted to a rootstock in a nursery and then planted. It takes three to five years from that point before they start producing. Soy should produce the first year you plant and every year after. Hydroponic systems require a set-up time, but typically a first harvest can be achieved in 18 months or less, depending on the system and the food being grown.

When Cash Flow Grows on Trees

The third type of agricultural investment for generating cash flow overseas is trees grown not for harvest but for timber.

Historically, timber has enjoyed the best risk/reward ratio of any investment sector. Depending on whose chart of historical returns you consult, timber as an asset category has produced an annualized ROI in the range of 12% to 15% per year every year since they started keeping records of investment risk versus return. It's a low-volatility hedge against inflation, an asset class that operates independent of the stock market, and a long-held secret of the world's wealthiest people.

Plus, timber is a commodity that will always have a market and that doesn't have to be harvested at a particular time. If prices for your wood are less than you want or expected them to be at the time you've planned to harvest, you can leave your trees in the ground so they can continue to grow until prices reach a level you like better.

The reluctance historically to investing in teak among small investors has been twofold: first, the investment required, and second, the long timeline to return.

Even a relatively small timber project requires significant capital. One colleague invested in a 100-acre teak plantation in Panama with six friends. The land buy was affordable, but the costs of planting and maintenance were multiples of that initial capital outlay.

Fortunately, in recent years, timber plantation developers have created projects that allow small investors to buy in. Again, in Europe, you'll be buying the trees, not the land. In Panama, some teak plantations offer direct land ownership. Some offer shares of a company. Buy where you own the land or the trees.

Timber holdings are a preferred investment for many pension and college endowment funds, because they like stable, low risk to reward investments and they have the time to wait for the returns.

For our money, teak is about the surest timber investment you can make. It is indigenous to only four countries—Burma, Thailand, Laos, and India. For centuries, the kings of Burma and Thailand considered teak a royal tree. Today, Burma, home to the last remaining natural teak forests, all of which are the property of the government, is the largest global exporter of premium teak. These remaining natural forests are being logged at a rapid rate, meaning the growing world demand (for outdoor furniture, flooring, boats, etc.) will have to be fulfilled by teak plantation production. And, right now, there aren't a lot of teak plantations worldwide.

Although trees take years rather than months to grow to a harvestable size, they also can carry less risk of being completely wiped out than, say, a soy crop. Teak trees have been farmed in plantations for hundreds of years starting with plantations in Southeast Asia. Today, teak plantations can be found in a band around the earth between 20 degrees north and 20 degrees south of the Equator. This includes Southeast Asia, India, Central America, Brazil, and parts of Africa. In addition to the required climate, you also need good soil to get decent growth rates for teak and a definitive dry season of at least four months. The dry season is when the hardwood in the center of the trees is made.

Taking a look at a world map and all things considered (the ideal growing requirements, the ease of investment, the cost of investment, the opportunities for investment, and the tax implications),

Panama jumps out as a top choice for investing in teak. This country is one of a handful of places in the world where you can grow premium teak trees. In addition, Panama is very pro-investor, home to a number of managed plantations, and, because it is interested in promoting forestry, makes the proceeds from related investments tax-free.

Owning a couple of hectares of teak trees could be a very profitable concept. At the same time, owning a couple of random hectares of any kind of tree doesn't make much investment sense. For this kind of investment to work, you need trees that are managed professionally by an outfit with both experience growing and harvesting the crop in question and access to a ready market for the end product. Few of us are prepared to invest the time that would be required to understand the industry and actually run the farm. We've known investors who have decided they didn't want to share proceeds with a management company and have chosen simply to plant some teak trees and left them to grow. The results have never been good. Teak trees need experienced care over their lifetimes to produce top-tier timber.

Fire is one key risk of a timber investment. Teak trees, however, are effectively immune from forest fires after about three years of growth. Years ago, we toured a timber plantation. The manager walked us through a section of the plantation where, a few years earlier, a wildfire had swept through. In that area at the time of the fire were four- and five-year-old plantings of cedar, mahogany, and teak. Almost all the cedar and mahogany trees were lost to the fire, but not one teak tree. We saw the teak growing still.

Insects are another risk. As with fire, though, teak is fairly immune after three years.

Perhaps the biggest drawback to investing in trees, teak or otherwise, is the investment term. Unlike cash crops, for example, which can mature in less than a year and be taken to market, you have to wait 10 to 25 years before you see any real return from a timber investment. Eucalyptus matures in maybe 13 years, pine in 15 to 20. It can take as long as 25 years before teak is ready for harvest, making it a good legacy investment, one you make as much for your kids and grandkids as for yourself. Thinnings are done several times during the growth cycle, but they bring limited cash flow. The full harvest is sometime between year 17 and year 25, depending on growth rates, which depend on soil and weather.

Top Tip from Kathleen

If you like the idea of investing in trees for timber but don't want to wait 25 years for a return from teak, consider a softwood plantation. Thanks to the growing demand for biofuel, these are increasingly common. A friend developing timber plantations in Colombia, for example, is planting acacia trees that will be harvested six or seven years after planting. The production is slated to be processed into biofuel pellets for electricity plants.

12

Fixer-upper—Make Money While Learning the Local History, Language, and Culture (If You Can Survive the Experience)

In 2012, we bought an apartment in Medellín, Colombia. It was nearly 400 square meters in an architecturally interesting building in a prime location and featured a terrace with an expansive view over the Medellín valley and the mountains beyond. It was a one-of-a-kind find.

But it was not the property we'd set out to buy. Our attention had been piqued by reports of annual net rental yields in this market of as much as 20%. We planned a scouting trip and looked at a dozen apartments that could have worked well as straightforward cash-flowing rentals generating that level of return, but it was the oversized apartment in El Poblado that got our attention. It was not rental ready, but the price was irresistible. It allowed us to buy at one of the best addresses in a market we predicted was positioned for rapid and dramatic capital appreciation, in addition to those 20% annual net yields, for the extraordinarily bargain price of $675 per square meter.

In addition, while the straight-up rentals we viewed were each more or less the same as all the others, this was a property of charm and character. At least it had the potential to be charming. The apartment had been the home of a single 80-year-old woman, who had lived in it alone for decades. The kitchen, the bathrooms, the fixtures, and the fittings were all 1950s originals. The place needed a total overhaul, meaning that, instead of a turnkey rental investment, we ended up opting for a gut-job rehab.

To carry it out, we engaged a local contractor named Carlos. With Carlos's help, we conceived a plan to reconfigure and rebuild the space. The apartment had a galley kitchen intended to be the domain of household help. We wanted a big, open kitchen with room for cooking and hanging out as a family. We also wanted a library, a game room, and a bar on the terrace.

The more we got into the project, the more personal it became. We imagined parquet floors in the living room and library, handmade and hand-painted Spanish-colonial tiles in the bathrooms and kitchen, and French doors to the terraces. We let our imaginations run because we'd been assured that the costs of this level of construction and finishing would be low. Both labor and materials were a screaming bargain … everyone told us.

We began the renovation in July. Carlos said the work would take four months. By late December, the place was still a wreck. By this point, we were concerned not only about the timeline but also the costs. We'd spent the total original budget, but the "Send more money" requests from Carlos were filling up our in-boxes and the photos he was sending to show progress didn't. We planned an emergency trip to Medellín to see what was what. Walking through the apartment with Carlos, we calmed down a bit. The demolition and behind-the-walls work had been done, and the new floors had been laid. Still, though, we had no doors, no windows, no bathroom fixtures, no bookcase in the library, no terrace bar, and no kitchen.

Four months of short fuses and heated email exchanges later, we walked through the front door of our finally remade El Poblado pad to find the sun beaming through the windows of the French doors to the terrace and glistening off the polished parquet. It was everything we'd originally imagined it might be.

And, when the final accounting was done, the top-tier renovation had cost nearly twice what we'd budgeted but was still a per-square-meter bargain, given the end result.

We've renovated 13 properties in six countries. The first thing we've learned is that they all, like the Medellín project, take twice as long and cost twice as much as you plan. We've not yet taken the step of allowing for this by doubling our time and expense projections from the outset. We worry that, if we did, the inflated figures would still fall short of the ultimate actual figures by half.

The reason the Medellín project stands out in memory is because, after renovating so personally, we were reluctant to rent. We listed the apartment with one, a second, and then a third rental management agency, but it rented maybe a total of six times. Fit a place out with custom parquet, hand-painted tiles, a claw-foot tub, and antique chandeliers and you become discriminating about who you feel comfortable allowing to spend the night. We set the rental rates so high that we priced ourselves out of the market. Finally, we pulled the listing from the third agency and hired a property manager to take care of cleaning and paying the bills. It was no longer a cash-flowing asset but a straight-up expense.

You could call it a rental investment disaster story. On the other hand, the apartment is now worth four times what we paid for it. It generates no rental cash flow, but we use the property for family vacations at least once a year. Kathleen is happy with the situation; Lief less so. It's perhaps our best example of what we've come to refer to as "The Spousal Effect." Lief's spreadsheet rental projections were out the window when Kathleen took charge of the project. What short-term tourist rental renovation budget includes custom cabinetry and leather Chesterfield sofas?

The third thing, therefore, that we've learned about undertaking a renovation project in a foreign country is that everyone involved must agree on the objective from the start. Is the completed property intended for rental or for personal use? Often the answer can be both, which is when things can get messy.

At some point during every renovation project we've taken on, we've sworn it's the last. Yet, even now, we'd tackle another under the right circumstances. First, a fixer-upper can be a bargain, allowing you to enter a property market at a low price and positioning you for potentially big capital appreciation upside in addition to, if you don't overdo or overdecorate, rental cash flow.

In addition, and for us more important, this is one of the best ways we've found to engage with the local community. In Ireland, France, Panama, Colombia, Argentina, and Portugal, the places where we've taken on renovation projects, the architects, contractors, woodworkers, painters, and landscape designers we've worked with have become personal friends and have been our entrée to the local scene, giving us insights into the local culture we wouldn't have had otherwise.

When we think back on the renovation of the nineteenth-century Georgian Lahardan House in Waterford, Ireland, we remember the little bent Irishman with the screwdriver in the back pocket of his tweed trousers who was the first to tell us the place we'd just bought was riddled with rising damp (though he walked away and out the door before we were able to ask him to explain what that meant). We see the Welshman Liam hoisting four or five sacks of cement at a go without noticing. We laugh about the gardener Ian who we finally realized was living in his car but who built beautiful stone walls. And we remind ourselves of John the cabinetmaker who worked around the clock for two weeks so we'd have a kitchen in time for our first Christmas.

It's possible to renovate a property in a country where you're not living. In fact, only one of our projects—Lahardan House in Ireland—was undertaken in the place we called home. All the others have been managed long distance. The three renovations of apartments in Buenos Aires, Argentina, were handled completely by an architect contact. We didn't see the apartments until a year after the work had been completed because they were rented on annual leases, but the architect sent pictures on a weekly basis to update us on the progress. Material selections and furniture choices were agreed via email. The process was seamless, but we wouldn't recommend it. Ideally, you should plan to visit the project at least monthly during the renovation process. At critical stages, you may need to be present weekly or daily. If you're not living where the property is located, add travel costs to your budget.

Based on more than two decades of experience, here are the 12 things we wish someone had told us before we undertook our first renovation overseas…

1: Location Is Still King

As with any real estate purchase, location is the number-one priority. It's the only attribute of the property that you can't change, and it's especially important with a restoration project, especially if you intend to rent the place. Renters will overlook a multitude of sins for a good location. With a city property, for example, walkability should be a priority. You want a location that's nearby to restaurants, cafes, grocery shopping, and home supplies. Both potential resale buyers and renters will appreciate the convenience and the ability to stay in the property without having to invest in a car.

2: Identify Your Potential Resale Buyer or Renter

As when investing in any property for rental, do your best to imagine who your renter might be from the start, before beginning the restoration work. If your renter will likely be a traveling executive, you'll make different choices than if you think you might be renting to families with children. The differences have implications for both the work you do and the location you pick.

3: Check the Structural Basics

Verify that the house is structurally sound where it counts. Problems with the foundation or structural members or termite-damaged framing can be too expensive to make right. The perfect fixer-upper has a solid structure but horrible curb appeal—an overgrown yard, peeling paint, and broken windows, for example. These are nickel and dime items that, when addressed, change the eventual value dramatically.

4: Set Your Target Budget in Keeping with the Surrounding Market

Before making a purchase, be sure that values in the neighborhood where you're considering buying are in line with what you imagine for your restoration project in its finished condition. Say you want to buy a house for $50,000, invest another $50,000, then ultimately resell the property for $150,000 (a reasonable expectation for profit margin). Before committing to the purchase, make sure other homes in the neighborhood are selling in that price range.

When making an offer on a fixer-upper that you intend to resell, start by estimating the price you'll eventually ask for the finished product at resale time. Then estimate the restoration costs (with help from local contractors if necessary). Add the total restoration costs to the purchase price to confirm that you're below the eventual asking price you imagine. A good rule of thumb is for your total investment (purchase price and renovation costs) to be at least 20% less than your imagined resale price. This means you could resell immediately upon completion of the renovation for a profit without having to wait for the market to appreciate if you decide you don't want to.

5: Spend on Items That Produce a Return

It's easy to overspend on non–value-adding items. A modern kitchen, granite or ceramic counters, painting, and updated bathrooms are worth the money. These are things that make a difference in photographs, which are key in attracting renters, and that usually add more value at resale time than you spend on them. On the other hand, custom bookcases, high-end cabinetry, specialty hardware, and even a swimming pool—while nice upgrades—are expenditures that may not make sense depending on who you're planning to target for rental. A beautiful gourmet kitchen can be worthwhile in a rental property in an upscale neighborhood of Panama City, Panama, but not in a town like Loja, Ecuador, where everyone has a maid who does the cooking. Inevitably, you'll invest in some little luxuries along these lines, things that matter to you and that will make the place comfortable for your use. But keep track of these indulgences to be sure they don't erode your eventual return too dramatically.

6: As Much as Possible, Go Local for Materials and Methods

In the United States and Canada, wood is cheap and plentiful. This is true in some other countries, as well (Belize, for example), but not all. In most of Latin America, lumber is expensive and rarely used as a bulk building material. To keep costs down (and also to ensure a solid home), plan on using masonry. Save the wood for trim. Local craftsmen in Ecuador, for example, build kitchen cabinets out of brick and ceramic tile then finish with wooden doors.

Try not to be too directive until you're familiar with how things are done locally. Each renovation project is a chance to learn new methods for construction. Fieldstone driveways, adobe and rammed-earth construction, and homemade clay tile roofs aren't typical in the United States, but they're the norm in many other countries, meaning these can be the most affordable options as well as the techniques local craftsmen are most familiar with.

7: Be There While the Work Is Going On

Even going out for lunch can be risky.

The difference between your standards and expectations and those of your contractor and workmen can be so vast as to defy explanation. You need to be prepared for this gap. It doesn't mean the workmen you've hired are bad at what they do; it means they do things differently.

As much as possible, be onsite when work is going on. If you can't be physically present yourself, you need to engage a trusted associate who knows your standards for quality, ideally another expat. If you hand a project over to a local craftsman or contractor, you're sure to find unwelcome surprises when you return.

8: Have the Money Before You Start the Work

Be sure you have the time and money to complete the project, assuming it's going to take longer and cost more than you're projecting. It always does.

9: Vet the Contractor

Take the time to investigate his track record and reputation before committing. Your contract is only as good as the person with whom you enter into it. In addition, insist that your contractor present you with a detailed itemized bid based on the architectural plans that includes everything from window and door frames to iron railings and zinc-plated screws.

10: Invest in Plans

Don't skimp on the architectural plans. You get what you pay for. We worked with one of the most expensive in Panama to draft the design for the house we built on the coast of Panama. We could have saved a few thousand dollars at least by using someone else, but we've seen how wrong things can go when the plans aren't fully thought-through and painstakingly detailed. When working in a foreign country with workers of varying levels of experience and expertise, it's a risk to leave anything open to interpretation. The crew on the ground has no choice but to improvise. We promise you that their improv will not meet your expectations.

11: Consider the Geography

If you're building at the coast, remember the toll that sun and sea air take. For our house at the beach in Panama, we used local hardwoods for finish details and treated the wood with wax, knowing that we'd have to reapply the wax finish often. It will be a constant part of the maintenance of the property. We invested in oversized rain gutters because, during the rainy season in this part of this country, the rain falls in torrents, and we built in extra insulation beneath our red clay-tiled roof to help control air-conditioning costs.

12: Always Hold Back Partial Payment

Don't pay in full up front for anything. You know this. It's common sense. However, we've gotten into trouble when we've listened to workers' hard-luck stories. Pay something to get the work in question underway, something more at agreed-upon progress benchmarks, and the final amount after all punch list items have been addressed. Don't be tempted to compromise on that plan.

IV

World's Top Cash Flow Markets—Where to Buy Whether You Have $50,000, $250,000, or $1 Million to Invest

After 64 property purchases over 30 years in 23 countries, we've found that it's possible to make a good property buy anywhere at any time if you look long and hard enough and have the experience and judgment to filter. However, on any particular day, it's easier to buy right in some places rather than others, and now and then we find a market where anyone could buy anything and profit.

Where should you consider buying?

If you're a retiree- or lifestyle-buyer shopping for a piece of property overseas that will generate cash flow when you're not using it yourself, the answer to the question is obvious. Direct your search according to your personal agenda. Where do you want to be? Target the country and the city where you'd like to spend time and then shop for a property with rental potential in that location.

If you're an investor buying strictly for cash flow, your challenge is greater. Following are the six best ways we've found to identify your top market options.

Top Tip from Kathleen

Here are the six factors to consider as you evaluate any market for potential investment:

Economic Outlook. Markets move up and down and then up again. At what point in this cycle is the market where you're thinking about buying right now? In which direction is it moving and why? If the market is moving up quickly because of foreign buyers (think the Spanish *costas* up until 2008), can you expect that foreign interest to continue? If not, who else might your eventual buyer be? Also, is there a reasonable expectation for appreciation in property values? If so, in what time frame—short, medium, or long term?

Inventory Supply and Demand. In expanding markets, supply typically takes time to catch up with demand, helping to create peaks and valleys in pricing even if the overall trend is up. In Panama City, right now, for example, a glut of high-rise condos is coming online. These units were launched and sold preconstruction over the past half-dozen years. Now they're being delivered, and their volume is one reason Panama's capital city's market continues soft.

The Path of Progress. Easier and better access opens up locations to broader markets. Therefore, one way to choose a market for investment is to identify a place where some important infrastructure improvement is planned. A new airport, new train station, new highway, new hospital, etc., can mean a new universe of potential buyers, and a newly paved road, for example, that cuts travel time in half, can make a location more accessible and therefore more valuable. All these things can translate into both expanding pools of potential renters and an exit strategy when the time comes.

Opportunity for Diversification. In terms of market, type of investment, type of property, and currency, a rental apartment in Medellín gives you an asset in Colombia that could generate cash flow in Colombian pesos. An agricultural investment in Brazil means another asset type, another economy, another currency, and so forth. The important thing to understand on the topic of diversification is that owning different kinds of properties in different cities and states across the United States isn't diversification. It's being invested in the United States.

However, neither is moving all your real estate investment capital out of the United States and placing it in any other single market—Panama, for example, or Colombia, or Brazil. Many investors we speak with recognize that holding property investments in two or three different U.S. cities means they are still fully exposed and vulnerable to U.S. market and U.S. dollar risks. Many, though, don't see that selling off all U.S. assets and reinvesting the capital in property in a single other country—even if, again, in different kinds of properties in different cities or locations throughout that single other country—is a similarly vulnerable position.

The point of diversification is to make sure you are not at the mercy of any single market, economy, political landscape, government, or currency. A global property diversification strategy could or could not include investments in the United States, but it must include investments in at least two (and preferably at least three) countries, ideally each with its own currency.

Note that not all foreign property markets bring currency diversification, because some countries use the U.S. dollar (Panama and Ecuador); some peg their currencies to the U.S. dollar (Belize); and, in some countries, though they have their own currency, real estate is traded in U.S. dollars (Nicaragua and some parts of Mexico), meaning that your currency hedge isn't as clean as it could be.

Also note that, while currency diversification can be one big benefit of investing in real estate overseas, we don't recommend you go chasing it. That is, don't try to time a property purchase based on moving exchange rates, not long term and not in the short term either. It's impossible to know which way any currency is going to move against any other currency day-to-day or month-to-month. Meantime, while you're trying to time the currency, the property market is moving, too.

If you know that you're interested in a particular market and the local currency takes a sudden hit, you could take that opportunity to move money in anticipation of making a buy. However, waiting for the currency to do what you want it to do, you run the risk of missing out on a good investment just because the time isn't "right" from a currency point of view. You can't time when you'll find the piece of property that you're searching for unless you don't allow yourself to begin looking until the currency moves to where you want it. That's a backward approach. Much better to lock in a good deal on a property than worry too much about a few percentage points on a currency move that may or may not happen according to your timeline.

Costs of Acquisition and Disposal. Remember that these, which we refer to as the "round-trip costs" of making an investment, go beyond agent commissions and vary dramatically country to country. This is an important thing to research and understand in full no matter why you're making a purchase; however, the investor–buyer who underestimates or underplans for the costs of acquisition and of eventually reselling can undermine his investment before he makes it. Depending on the market, the costs of purchasing a piece of real estate in another country can include, in addition to agent commissions: legal fees, notary fees, registration fees, title insurance, and transfer taxes (sometimes called "stamp duty"). In Ireland, for example, stamp duty was as much as 9% of the purchase price when we bought, payable in cash upon closing and not a cost you wanted to overlook in your budgeting. (Today it's 1% if the purchase price is less than 1 million euros.)

Again, though, remember, we're talking not only about the costs of acquisition, but the round-trip costs of a purchase. Exiting comes at a cost, too. When selling, you may have another agent commission to pay, and you'll likely have additional attorney fees. These are usually minimal, even negligible. The more significant cost associated with exiting a foreign property investment can be the tax hit. We discuss strategies for how to figure and how to minimize this in Appendix D.

The total round-trip costs of investing in a piece of real estate overseas can range from a few percentage points to more than 25% at the extreme and that can be before taking into account capital gains taxes. These costs shouldn't keep you out of a market where you want to invest, but they definitely should be taken into account in your budget.

Carrying Costs. Including maintenance (a house on the beach requires a lot of it); a caretaker (if necessary); property taxes (not every country charges them, and, in some countries, they're negligible); income taxes (if you're earning rental income); capital gains taxes (when you eventually resell—again, not every country charges them); other local taxes; rental and property-management expense; and homeowner's association/building/condo fees.

13 Where a Strong Dollar Creates Opportunity

If you're holding U.S. dollars, you have a window of opportunity right now to take advantage of super-charged buying power in key overseas markets. The dollar's current strength is creating irresistible bargains in some countries where real estate trades in the local currency. We refer to this temporary distortion (no one can predict how long it will last but you can be sure it won't continue forever) as a "currency discount." It's a metric we watch closely, and it amounts to a big, bold "Buy!" signal.

The difference of a percentage point or two in the rate at which one currency is able to buy another isn't going to change your lifestyle day to day, but, when buying property, even 1% can start to look like real money.

To put the current opportunity into perspective, the U.S. dollar is up a whopping 83% versus the Brazilian real, for example, since 2011.

Strong Dollar Buy #1: Brazil

Brazil is perhaps the world's best beachfront buy. How many places worldwide can you buy on the beach for $100,000 or less? That's the potential in Brazil, where beachfront property is not only super cheap but also ultra in demand. That bargain-priced beach house or apartment could earn you a double-digit net yield from rental.

Part of the reason beachfront can be so affordable is the country has so much of it, so you need to be discriminating. Don't settle for just any of Brazil's beaches. Research the rental demand and who your buyer might be when you decide you'd like to sell. Brazil has a huge internal tourism market fueled by its fast-growing middle class. The best buy is one that could appeal to both the local and also the expanding foreign-tourist demand. We like Fortaleza because it checks this box and its beaches are world-class.

Culturally, Brazil is one step beyond Latin America. The lifestyle and the language are more unfamiliar than elsewhere in the region and therefore more exotic and romantic. In parts, the climate is warm year-round; elsewhere changing, with seasons opposite those in the Northern Hemisphere. Culturally, Brazil is Germanic in the south, with French and Dutch influences up north.

One downside to Brazil can be its renowned bureaucracy. You might hear stories of foreign investors unable to get their money out of Brazil when trying to take their exits. Invariably, in our experience, these investors were either ignorant of or chose to ignore the process for registering investment funds when they brought theirs into the country. You need to follow the rules, filing the proper paperwork, to be sure you can repatriate your funds when you sell. The country's currency controls shouldn't put you off, but you must take the associated process seriously.

Historically, Americans and Canadians needed a visa to enter Brazil as a tourist. This was an annoying process that cost time and money. In July 2019, Brazil dropped all visa requirements for Americans and Canadians, making it that much easier for us to visit the country. Also, in 2019, Brazil introduced a new realestate-for-residency option. In Northeast Brazil, the region of the country we like best for a cash-flow investment, the minimum purchase to qualify for permanent residency is 700,000 reals, which is about $188,000 at today's exchange rate. (Check xe.com for today's exchange rate.)

Brazil is more accessible than it's ever been. This is a long, stretched-out country, and, previously, you had to route through Rio de Janeiro or Sao Paolo in the south to get anywhere in the country, including anywhere in the north. Today it's possible to fly direct from North America and Europe to Brazil's major regional capitals.

Strong Dollar Buy #2: Colombia

When we purchased our apartment in Medellín in 2011 and reported on the experience to our *Live and Invest Overseas* readers, one wrote in to tell us we were "foolish" to be buying property in Colombia at the then-exchange rate of around 1,800 pesos to US$1. He was going to wait to buy until the exchange rate hit his target of 3,000 to the dollar. More than four years later, the peso finally fell to 3,000 to US$1. However, property values in Medellín had risen 40% or more in the same period. If the guy who'd written in to chastise us was still looking at property in Medellín in 2015, when the exchange rate hit his target, he would have been able to buy a property for maybe 10% less in U.S. dollars than he could have in 2011. Meantime, he'd missed out on four years of cash flow and personal use.

For us, the exchange rate didn't matter. We saw Medellín as a buy, a market we wanted in on. We found and purchased an apartment that we still own. Today it's worth three times what we paid for it in pesos; in U.S. dollars, it's a double. In addition, we have had use of the property all these years and look forward to every chance to return. For our money, Medellín, Colombia, offers the best city living in the Americas. Its El Poblado neighborhood, where our apartment is located, is pretty, clean, safe, and pleasant, with shady streets, upscale shopping, and lots of restaurants, cafes, and parks.

Short-term rental yields in Medellín were an impressive 15% to 18% net when we bought into the market, but that lasted only a few years. Markets always revert to the mean. Today, rental yields in Medellín fall into our target range of 5% to 8% net, but other Colombian markets have stronger cash-flow potential, including Santa Marta on the Caribbean coast.

Property prices in cities across Colombia can be expected to appreciate at a nice clip for the foreseeable future, thanks to the country's growing middle class, and short-term rental yields are strong in many markets due to improving tourism numbers. The clincher right now is that, at the current exchange rate of 3,300 pesos to the dollar (again, check current rates online), you could well be buying at a currency top. Your strong dollar will go far in peso terms, and then the asset could appreciate with the support of a strengthening Colombian peso.

For the record and in case you harbor concerns, Pablo Escobar was killed in 1993, FARC has laid down its weapons, and Colombia has enjoyed one of the strongest economies in Latin America for the past decade.

In addition, Colombia now qualifies as one of the easiest places to obtain residency. You have 17 visa options to choose from, and qualifying requirements are minimal. A friend obtained Colombian residency in less than an hour at the ministry in Bogota following the instructions on the government's website. He managed the process on his own, without the help of an attorney. We don't recommend that approach even if you, like our friend, speak fluent Spanish, but you get the point. Colombia is working hard to make itself as user-friendly as possible for the would-be foreign investor and retiree.

Strong Dollar Buy #3: Euroland

Most American investors and retirees ignore Europe even if that's the part of the world where they'd most like to spend their time and money, assuming they can't afford it. Today's strong dollar creates a window of opportunity in euroland. Paris and Florence might be beyond the typical buyer's budget, but the 24 countries where real estate trades hands in euro are more affordable today than they've been in years.

The euro has been trading in the range of $1.10 to $1.15 since the beginning of 2015. From 2010 until 2015, the exchange rate moved in the range of $1.20 to $1.45. Between the high and the low of those ranges are 24 percentage points of added buying power that your dollars currently enjoy.

We put Portugal and Spain at the top of the list of euro-property investment markets. Other options to consider for euro-based cash flow include France and Italy and capital cities Prague and Budapest; all have strong short-term rental potential.

Depending on your personal agenda, small villages in France and Italy can be irresistible, both in terms of the lifestyle they offer and the cost of buying into it. Markets in parts of rural Italy are so depressed that local mayors are offering old properties in need of restoration for as little as 5,000 euro. At today's exchange rate, that's not much more in dollar terms. These locations would have limited cash-flow potential and small resale pools. Still, if you like the idea of Italian country living and are up for a renovation adventure, this is a moment of opportunity.

Elsewhere in Europe can be a great choice for combining the investment and lifestyle aspects of owning real estate overseas. Busy tourist markets allow you to organize your schedule to spend the off-season in Europe, and then rent the place for cash flow when demand surges. Combine a seasonal rental in Europe with another in another part of the world where the high season is some time of year other than European summer (this would include all of Central America and the Caribbean, where the high season is December through March), and you've created a diversified portfolio that should generate year-round cash flow. Meantime, you've eliminated housing cost from your budget, because you're living in your own properties.

Remember Schengen rules. These allow you to spend only up to 90 days in a rolling 180-day period in most EU countries. This means you can spend up to three months at a time in Europe without going through the process to qualify for legal residency.

14   Where Tourists Rule

The most obvious place to target for your first overseas property buy is an active tourist market. Not only is it easier to project and to feel confident of rental cash flow in a market with a track record, but active markets have established management industries and infrastructure, making it easier to connect with a rental manager and to outfit your purchase for rental.

We've made the point elsewhere, but it's worth repeating. Favor markets where demand is diversified. A market completely reliant on either foreign or local tourists is riskier than one that draws good numbers of both.

Another key to choosing right when shopping for a tourist rental can be avoiding cookie cutter and opting for something with inherent value. Beachfront is always a winner. Properties within walking distance of local amenities and a golf course also stand out even in a competitive marketplace. Whatever you do, don't buy an apartment in a complex of 300 identical apartments. You're reduced to competing for tenants on price and could find yourself one of a dozen or more owners trying to sell the same product at the same time when you decide to take your exit. Again, the only way to entice a buyer to choose your unit over all the others available for sale would be to lower the price.

Top Tourist Rental Buy #1: Mexico

You know that North Americans like to travel to Mexico to escape winter. Mexico's growing middle class likes to spend time on the country's beaches, too. Hot spots like Cancun and Puerto Vallarta rely on North American tourists to fill resorts November through February. Mexican tourists keep occupancy rates up during the summer months.

Our top tourist beach rental pick in this country is Playa del Carmen, the little beach town about an hour south of Cancun on Mexico's Riviera Maya. Once a sleepy fishing village, the port was inadvertently put on the map by Jacques Cousteau in 1954 when he filmed an underwater documentary of the Great Mayan Reef just offshore Cozumel Island and about 12 miles out from

Playa del Carmen. Divers began seeking out these Caribbean waters, and, in the 1970s, a port was built to ferry tourists from the mainland to Cozumel. In the years to follow, Playa del Carmen ("Playa" to the locals) became more globally known, but only as an access point to Cozumel, the real star.

Simultaneously, 35 miles to the north, Fondo Nacional de Fomento Turismo (FONATUR), the Mexican government agency charged with targeting stretches of this country's long and sunny coasts for development, was doing its thing in Cancun. FONATUR's efforts in Cancun were so successful that it wasn't long before tourists to that northern point on this Riviera Maya coast reached critical mass and began looking for less crowded beaches. They discovered Playa, about an hour south, which, as a result, by the early 1990s, became the fastest-growing city in Mexico. Today's Riviera Maya is responsible for 30% of the country's tourism income, and Playa, named many times by TripAdvisor as the top destination in Mexico, plays a key role. The best rentals are on the water and along La Quinta Avenida (Fifth Avenue), the pedestrianized street that runs parallel to the beach.

The biggest downside to Mexico can be safety. This is a big country, and, yes, drug cartels make certain areas, especially along the U.S. border, no-go zones both for living and for investing. However, the cartels tend to avoid tourist zones. In fact, that's one reason the Mexican tourist market has expanded along the Yucatan Riviera Maya coast. Mexicans find it safe to vacation there.

Another benefit of Mexico, especially for a first-time overseas investor, is that it's close to home. You can get to Cancun, the nearest access point for Playa del Carmen, via quick direct flights from many U.S. cities. Thanks to this easy access, Playa attracts not only foreign tourists but also foreign retirees and second-home buyers, meaning a diversified market for renters and potential buyers when you're ready to resell.

Mexico is another market benefiting from the surging U.S. dollar. Dollar buyers have 50% more buying power in this country today than they did in 2013. Note, though, that real estate in some Mexican markets, including Playa, trades in U.S. dollars. Also note that some U.S. banks offer U.S. dollar mortgages for the purchase of property in Mexico and that some Mexican banks lend locally to nonresident North American buyers.

Top Tourist Rental Buy #2: Spain

Spain is the Florida of Europe. This is where retirees from Northern Europe head in their old age. It's also a top destination among EU snowbirds and vacationers. Decades of demand from tourists and retirees from the UK, Germany, the Netherlands, and Scandinavia created a boom market on this Mediterranean coast that became one of the greatest casualties of the 2008 global real estate crisis. Property prices in some parts of Spain dropped by as much as 75%, and values along the *costas* fell 50% overnight. Some markets are only recovering now, more than a decade later. Overconstruction, including construction by rogue developers without proper permits, along with epic lending at variable rates, created bloating that led to absolute collapse.

Many developments, especially along the coast, went into foreclosure, and you still can find properties coming off lenders' books. Great buys are possible, and this is a proven, perennial cash-flow market. Just as Americans will always migrate to Florida in search of sunshine, North Europeans will continue to make their way to Spain's Mediterranean coast for the same reason. The secret to successful buying for cash flow in this market is location. This is true for any property purchase anywhere but sometimes especially critical. This is one of those times. Each Spanish *costa* is different from all the others.

Most famous is the Costa del Sol. Puerto Banus attracts the rich and famous. The slightly less rich can be found in nearby Marbella. Retirees stretch along the coast toward Gibraltar. Many of the individual *costas* have tourist markets, as well, but remember to avoid the ubiquitous complexes.

That is not to say to dismiss ugly. Some of Spain's Mediterranean coast was developed in the 1960s and 1970s. The beachfronts of towns like Benidorm and Torremolinos are dense with old resorts and high-rise buildings. Although they can be unattractive, as most 1960s and 1970s architecture all over the world is, these legacy projects are also the best located. They're more limited in supply than the apartments built in more recent decades and better positioned. These granddaddy properties can generate strong yields.

Beachfront can be the surest short-term rental to buy, but real estate in a brand-name city can hold its value while generating reliable cash flow, too. Barcelona is such a city. Prices are higher than along the coast on a per-square-meter basis because values in Barcelona didn't fall as far during the crisis as those on the overbuilt *costas,* thanks to more limited supply and local demand.

One thing to note when investing in rental property in Spain is that the Spanish assume that, if a property you own is not your primary residence, you're renting it out. As a nonresident property owner in Spain, you will get a tax bill each year based on a presumed level of rental income. It's Spain's way of guaranteeing itself payment of tax on rental income earned by foreigners, who, for decades, didn't report it. Now the Spanish figure it for you, so, if you buy a second home in Spain, you might as well rent it when you're not using it yourself. You're going to be taxed as though you are regardless.

Top Tip from Kathleen

When looking for property along the Spanish *costas* or the Algarve in Portugal, don't expect real estate agents to know anything about markets beyond their immediate areas. Agents typically don't cover more than a few miles up or down the coast from the towns where they are based. Some agencies cover a broader area, but that's not common, so it's a good idea to narrow your search radius according to your personal criteria before you begin knocking on real estate agents' doors. You'll need either to do your homework in advance or embrace the inefficient and extended search process as an adventure and a chance to discover different areas along these countries' coasts.

Top Tourist Rental Buy #3: Portugal

Portugal followed a path similar to that of Spain in the wake of the 2008 real estate crisis. Property prices fell as much as 50% across the country. The difference was that Portugal wasn't nearly as overbuilt as Spain, so most markets recovered more quickly.

On the other hand, Portugal has never had the same tourist or retiree appeal as Spain. Almost 83 million foreign tourists traveled to Spain in 2018, while Portugal saw but 12.8 million visitors that year.

Development along Portugal's coast never reached the levels of development along the coast of Spain because, since the early 1990s, Portugal has restricted it. No new construction is allowed within 500 meters of the water, and new construction anywhere in coastal regions comes with height limitations. This has kept Portugal's coast largely free of the high-rises and massive condo projects that blight the Mediterranean shores of Spain. Portugal has a few bona-fide international resort towns (Albufeira, for example), packed with tourists and their trappings each season, but even these feel cozy compared with some of Spain's tackiest locales.

The downside to the Algarve region is that it's relatively small. It compares in size to a single one of the Spanish *costas*. That makes it more manageable from a research and property shopping perspective but also means more limited investment options. Real estate values in many of the hottest tourist spots on the Algarve coast increased significantly between 2015 and 2019, pushing down rental yields. Lagos, for example, was an undervalued market when we purchased our apartment there, but we wouldn't recommend focusing on this city now.

Lesser-known areas haven't seen the same levels of appreciation but also don't see the same volume of tourists each season. Look to the eastern half of the Algarve for the best buys. We particularly like Taveira.

Lisbon has seen tremendous appreciation since 2015, as well as a significant increase in tourism. Prices per square meter in key tourist neighborhoods have pushed past those in central Barcelona, but Lisbon can still make sense if your budget stretches to afford it. The best buy today could be a renovation project outside the known hot spots of Barrio Alto, Chiado, and Baixa.

For a city cash-flow buy, we also like Porto, just beginning to attract attention. As in Lisbon, the best investments are on the edges of the city center, in neighborhoods where tourists don't need a car to get around.

Top Tip from Lief

We're focusing your attention on three proven tourist destinations, but the world holds many others, and new viable cash-flow markets are always emerging. When you begin your search for a tourist rental, consider the whole world map in that moment. However, make sure any new market you consider has the legs to continue attracting tourists long term and isn't a passing fad.

15

Where You Can Buy Preconstruction to Flip or Rent

Buying to flip is a common real estate investment strategy in the United States that doesn't make sense in most of the rest of the world where leverage isn't easy and the costs of buying and selling are typically too great to make the math work.

The option is to buy preconstruction.

New construction is ongoing in most active real estate markets, meaning developers are constantly looking for help funding next projects. One strategy can be for them to presell units in planned buildings. The developer generates cash flow, and you, as the investor, benefit from a reduced price and staged payments.

The biggest advantage for you as the buyer is the ability to flip your unit, if the market sticks with you, before having to come up with the big final payment when construction is complete. This is both the greatest upside and a risk. If you're not able to sell before that final payment is due, you could lose everything. That's why we don't recommend a preconstruction investment if you don't have the cash to close. Have enough capital in reserve to cover all payments before entering into a preconstruction contract.

Not that you're going to close with your own capital if you can help it. For this kind of investment, focus on markets where financing is possible—either from a bank or the developer—so you have a backup for that final payment and save your own cash for other opportunities.

Top Buy-to-Flip Market #1: Panama

All Panama but especially Panama City has been one of the greatest economic success stories of the past two decades. The massive growth has been due largely to foreign investment.

When the United States handed over ownership of the Panama Canal to Panama in 1999, the country fell immediately into recession. It needed to find a way to replace the disposable income that all those U.S. GIs had been spreading around and quick. The country looked next-door to Costa Rica, whose economy is based almost entirely on income from foreign tourists and resident retirees. We could do that, too, Panama figured, and began working in earnest to attract the attention of North Americans.

Panama targeted eco-tourists and budget-conscious Baby Boomers looking for places where they could stretch their retirement nest eggs. It introduced a *pensionado* residency program, improving on the model Costa Rica had by now made famous, offering resident retirees discounts on everything from restaurant tabs and movie tickets to plane fares and prescription medications. Retirees, Panama figured, like the American GIs, living in the country, would be spending on a monthly basis. Tourists, while helpful for an economy, come and go.

Next, Panama targeted international companies, playing up the incomparable advantage of its geographic position. This country literally at the hub of the Americas is ideally located for a business doing business across the Americas. Plus, thanks to the investment made over decades by the U.S. military, the infrastructure in Panama City is in a league of its own for the region, and much of the population, thanks again to the extended American presence, is English-speaking. Panama wooed companies like Dell, Proctor & Gamble, Adidas, Caterpillar, Nike, Estee Lauder, and others shopping for the best place to locate their regional headquarters. Today, more than 150 multinational corporations have this country's capital as their base, employing, among them, thousands, including hundreds of foreign management staff. All these people need places to live, and the imported foreign executives have helped fill buildings that many predicted would sit empty long after completion.

Panama has a second incomparable advantage in its canal, which it expanded in 2016 and which generates more than $2.6 billion of revenue each year. That's a lot of cash flow for a country of 4.2 million people, and the amount increases every year. Panama wisely continues to invest much of this canal income into infrastructure projects, expanding its highway systems, building new hospitals, and generally making the country ever more appealing for the foreign investor. Coupled with its developed international banking and financial services industries, the canal economy has helped to position Panama as a regional safe haven.

Colombians, Venezuelans, and Argentines like to park their capital in Panama City's dollar-denominated condos, fueling the city's preconstruction market.

Now Panama has attracted another pool of foreign investors—the Chinese. In June 2017, former President Juan Carlos Varela ended diplomatic relations with Taiwan and established formal ties with Beijing, leading to a tidal wave of Chinese investment. China is positioned to become Panama's most important commercial partner. Mega-infrastructure projects under discussion include a new rail system to make the transport of goods from the west of the country to the canal more efficient.

In separate good economic news, in 2019, the country began development of the largest copper mine in the world, setting the stage for a new source of significant revenues long term.

In the 20 years since the Americans pulled out, Panamanian markets have cycled, including a drop in property prices after the 2008 global crisis, but the trajectory has been and continues up. We first recommended Panama's property market as a buy in 1998 and are more bullish on this country's prospects today than ever. However, as we write, values are soft, creating a buy-on-the-dip opportunity.

The country's preconstruction market is established, extensive, and competitive, meaning many options. The best deals are the earliest in. Shop for a just-released building to get the biggest discount.

One developer we've worked with in this country for two decades offers medium-term financing for some units in some buildings. He can't make staged payments an option for all units or all buildings because then he wouldn't have enough capital for up-front construction costs. Still, his buy-over-time program gives him an advantage in the marketplace. No other developer in Panama offers such an option.

Historically, developers and investors in Panama have focused primarily on the upper end of the market. Panama City is home to a surprising number of $1 million-plus apartments. That buyer is well catered to.

Recently, another developer we've worked with for years has identified a new niche—the Panamanian yuppie. All those international companies hiring all that management staff are creating a new demographic, a high-end subset of the local middle class. These people can't afford the million-dollar apartments on Avenida Balboa or in Punta Pacifica, but they don't want to live outside the city and commute two hours each way to work, creating a demand for small- to medium-sized apartments in internationally competitive buildings in central city locations. This developer is offering good preconstruction terms for units in buildings that should appreciate in value while generating solid cash flow.

Top Buy-to-Flip Market #2: Dominican Republic

Rapidly expanding demand and undervalued pricing make the Dominican Republic (DR) a top rental investment market, and local developers are looking to fund new projects through preconstruction. You can buy a rentable apartment for as little as $100,000 or less. One-bedroom units in a project in a prime Santo Domingo location that we're analyzing as we write this book start at $66,000. Financing is possible for foreign buyers, meaning the DR offers the lowest buy-in capital requirement of any cash-flow market we know. A modest investment positions you for net yields as high as 10% per year.

Having invested in a rental property in the DR, you'll have no trouble filling it. The number of tourists visiting these shores has increased year over year for the past decade. The DR, which saw more than 7 million tourists in 2019, growth of 8% over the previous year, is the top destination in the Caribbean, representing 20% of travel to the region.

The country's open-sky policy has resulted in many new flights, including more nonstop routes to and from the United States. All those arriving passengers translate to average hotel occupancy rates of 77%. These tourism trends are expected to continue, fueling short-term rental demand, including both for beachfront resort communities with five-star amenities and for well-located executive rentals in capital city Santo Domingo.

The DR's burgeoning tourism economy is not reliant on one market. The country attracts travelers from North America, Europe, and South America, with direct flights from all three continents. Beaches are the main draw, but Santo Domingo adds one of the biggest and oldest Spanish-colonial town centers to the mix of attractions, and, as the country works to position itself as a Caribbean business hub, executive travelers are creating a new demand.

Specifically, we like the DR for a preconstruction buy for these reasons:

1. **Prices Represent the Best Value in the Caribbean**

   From real estate to the general cost of living, it can be hard to believe you're in the Caribbean. Prices are more Latin American. A retiree can live in the country on Social Security alone, creating growing demand from American retirees.

2. **The Established Expat Community Means Amenities and Services You Won't Find Elsewhere in the Caribbean**

   White-sand beaches, swaying palm trees, warm turquoise water, year-round sunshine—you'll find them in abundance in the DR, as well, of course, as everywhere else in the Caribbean. What sets the DR apart from other Caribbean islands is its more sophisticated, Euro-chic lifestyle. Santo Domingo, the oldest permanent European settlement in the New World, boasts impressive Spanish-colonial architecture, along with modern shopping options, theaters, museums, and sports stadiums. *Béisbol* is a national obsession.

   In our favorite spots in this country, you don't have to worry about being the first expat in town. In Las Terrenas, for example, on the Samaná Peninsula, a large international community will welcome you, and you'll enjoy access to a wide range of products from patisserie-baked *pain au chocolat* to authentic German sausage. If you like the idea of a European life but would rather be within a two-hour hop of the U.S. East Coast (and enjoying better weather than in most of Europe), Las Terrenas could be the paradise you're looking for.

3. **Infrastructure Improvements Make for an Improving Quality of Life**

   Recently upgraded airports mean you can get to the DR from the U.S. East Coast in two hours. On the island, new highways have cut journey times from the capital to other key locations by half and more. No more getting lost down dirt tracks or driving a painful six hours to reach the opposite coast.

This improving accessibility has helped to reduce day-to-day living costs. Food costs have fallen by as much as 30% in the last several years.

4. **Easy Retiree Residency**

The country is keen to compete with other countries offering retiree residency programs, offering perks, benefits, and tax breaks to those who qualify.

5. **The Government Is Rolling Out the Red Carpet for Investors and Entrepreneurs**

With its central location in the Americas, a fast-developing infrastructure, and a generous program of tax incentives, the DR is making a name for itself as one of the best places in the Caribbean to do business. The government welcomes foreign investors to its industrial free zones. If you have a business to transplant or are looking to set up your own business in a tax-friendly, benefit-laden location, you owe it to yourself to investigate the opportunities here—especially if your work falls under any of the following categories: telecommunications, infrastructure, renewable energy, agribusiness, call centers, software development, manufacturing, or tourism. Start up a business in a free-trade zone and, thanks to Law 8-90, you'll qualify for a 15-year exemption on income tax, corporate tax, VAT, municipal taxes, export tax and duties, and incorporation and capitalization taxes.

You don't have to be in big business to take advantage of the DR's tax incentives. The government is committed to tourism growth. It recognizes the potential in its coastlines, its jungles, and its historic capital city. Its big agenda is sustainable tourism, and it's rolling out the red carpet to those willing to help boost its tourism efforts. Start even a tiny tourism business here—a boutique hotel, a tour company, or a dive shop—and, under Law 158-01, you'll receive tax breaks for the next 10 years.

While the DR is a top market for a first-time buyer with a limited budget, bigger-ticket buys are available. Some of the country's beach resort towns attract higher-end tourists looking for luxury-level rentals. These probably don't make sense for a preconstruction flip strategy but could be purchased with local bank financing if your portfolio accommodates that level of investment in a single market.

Note that, despite the fancy beach resorts, modern shopping malls, and new high-rise buildings, the DR is still the developing world with developing-world challenges like poverty, corruption, and a generally inefficient approach to business. If you'll struggle in the face of those things, focus on other markets.

Top Buy-to-Flip Market #3: Poland

Our final buy-to-flip market is off most people's radar, both for investment and for lifestyle, but we like Krakow, Poland. This historic city is enjoying a growing tourism industry (with 10 million visitors in 2019) and is home to 10 universities, creating student rental demand. Buying preconstruction in Eastern Europe could be outside your comfort zone, but Krakow is a market with good potential that you could get into with less than $100,000.

Look for a project close to the old town or one of the universities. Krakow is a small city of only about 760,000 people, so its real estate market isn't as active or complex as, say, Panama City. If it sparks your interest, you'll be able to get a handle on the lay of the land quickly.

Many other destinations can make sense for a preconstruction flip. The key to success at this strategy is a buoyant economy where housing demand is expanding rapidly. That demand growth could be thanks to foreign workers or students moving to the city, as in Panama City and Krakow. Or it could be the result of a swelling middle class, meaning more local folks every month looking for bigger or more modern housing options.

16 Where You Can Leverage

everage is a key tool in every U.S. property investor's kit. As late-night TV real estate investment gurus with courses and programs to sell assure us, other people's money (OPM) is the secret to success building a real estate investment portfolio. In fact, OPM allowed Lief to take his first step onto the property ladder in Chicago, and we've been able to leverage investments (through bank financing, preconstruction terms, and seller carrybacks) in Ireland, France, Portugal, Spain, the UK, and Panama.

Leverage can make possible a purchase that wouldn't be otherwise, and it can improve your return on investment. It can also cost you everything if you're not able to keep up with required payments, as has happened to us. We recommend against borrowing to buy when you don't have a backup plan.

In much of the world, you're spared the risk. Bank financing isn't easily available for foreign investors in many overseas markets, "foreign" investors being the key point. If you're a resident in a country where you'd like to borrow for the purchase of real estate, as we were when we applied for bank financing in Ireland, your chances are the same as your local neighbors'. You qualify or not based on your financial circumstances. A bank looks on a foreigner as a much greater risk. It doesn't have the infrastructure to chase down loan repayments in another jurisdiction. A foreign buyer can simply walk away from his mortgaged property. That means losing the down payment but doesn't create long-term repercussions. Default on a mortgage at home, and your credit record carries that scar. Developing-world markets don't have the ability to track and report on these kinds of things, and you don't necessarily have to care about your credit history in Brazil or Belize, where, after walking away from a property with an outstanding loan, you can choose never to return. Local banks understand this.

Where can you qualify today for bank financing as a foreign buyer? Here are three options…

Top Market for Local Leverage #1: Panama

Banks in Panama are currently flush with cash. They are trying to push a credit card into the hand of every Panamanian with a bank account. Credit is too easy to get. The situation reminds us of Ireland when we moved to Waterford in 1998. The Celtic Tiger borrowing bubble finally burst in 2008, and we wonder how long the one in Panama will continue. However, we Americans aren't benefitting (or being put at risk, depending on your perspective). Banks in Panama are not so interested in dealing with us. The United States is throwing its weight around the world in the name of its anti–money-laundering crusade, but it's applying special pressure on Panama's banking system in response to the 2018 Mossack Fonseca scandal. It's possible to find a bank that will lend to you in Panama (assuming you qualify), but we hesitate to mention any specific bank to approach. They change their internal rules related to lending to Americans faster than you can take money out of one of their ATMs.

The terms for the rental property we financed in Panama in 2000 required a down payment of 20%. Panama banks willing to lend to nonresident buyers today will require a higher down payment. In fact, you're not likely to get an 80% loan-to-value ratio anywhere in the world today as a nonresident buyer or even as a legal resident if your income is derived from outside the country where you're looking to buy.

In addition to putting down at least 30% to get bank financing in Panama, you'll also have to buy a local life insurance policy naming the bank as beneficiary in the event of your death (as you'll be required to do in most countries), and your interest rate will be 1% higher than the going local rate. The interest rate surcharge is for mortgages on a second home or commercial property, and it's imposed by law rather than bank policy. When lending to you as a nonresident, the bank assumes that the property you're borrowing to buy won't be your primary residence. If you're moving to Panama and do plan to live in the property, explain this to the bank to avoid the extra 1% interest.

Even with the 1% surcharge, your mortgage rate won't be outrageous, but it will be higher than U.S. rates. Expect about 7%. The rate, whatever it is, will be variable, as fixed interest rates are uncommon outside the United States. This worries some borrowers, but, in the 13 years we've held our 25-year mortgage in Panama, the rate has been adjusted only once. It was increased 0.25%.

Panama banks use the same criteria as U.S. banks to assess your financial situation, including your U.S. credit score. They process payment and debt-to-income ratios in the same way with one critical difference. Panama banks consider the limit on any credit card as debt even if you're not carrying a balance on that card. It's an extremely conservative approach and creates problems even for Panamanians now that they all have credit cards, too.

One Panamanian we know was forced to pay off his credit cards and cancel them to obtain a mortgage, after which he was able to get new credit cards, including one from the bank who'd just given him a mortgage.

Top Market for Local Leverage #2: Portugal

Money is practically free in Europe if you qualify. European Central Bank (ECB) rates are so low that, when borrowing, you're simply paying the bank's margin, which can range from 1.5% to 2%.

Portugal is one European market where a nonresident foreigner can get a mortgage. The process is straightforward in theory, and it's possible even to request pre-approval from a bank before you've found the property you want to buy. However, if your income is from passive rather than active sources, you'll be required to provide more paperwork before final approval is granted.

If you're buying with the expectation of obtaining financing, make sure a contingency clause is included in your purchase agreement. Many sellers overseas don't like contingency clauses. You buy caveat emptor. The burden falls always on you as the buyer to carry out your own due diligence before signing a purchase agreement. So, when a mortgage is involved, even if you have a bank's pre-approval, insist on making the purchase contingent on your financing coming through. You can't take for granted that the bank will in fact lend to you after they have carried out the final review of your documentation.

A friend was pre-approved for a mortgage in Portugal only to find, after having signed a purchase agreement, that the bank wanted additional information regarding his income. He was retired, and all his income was passive. He could produce U.S. tax returns showing years of enough passive income to qualify for the amount he was asking to borrow, but the Portuguese bank wouldn't accept the tax returns as proof of income unless they were certified by the IRS. The IRS doesn't do that. In the end, our friend wasn't able to get financing, despite meeting the debt-to-income ratios and, again, despite having been pre-approved for the loan. He lost the down payment on the property he'd committed to buying.

Banks in Portugal will lend up to 60% to a nonresident borrower. Mortgage terms rarely exceed 25 years anywhere in the world, and that's the standard in Portugal (though it can be possible to persuade a bank to extend the term to 30 years, depending on your age).

Top Market for Local Leverage #3: Spain

Spanish banks follow lending rules similar to those in Portugal, and you'll find plenty willing to lend despite the hit so many took after the 2008 collapse and even though some are still cleaning up their foreclosed property lists. In fact, the financing industry is so sophisticated in Spain you might want to opt for a mortgage broker to help you find the best deal. You can engage one for as little as a 500-euro fixed fee. Do your research to make sure you won't end up paying any hidden fees via the bank. And, again, as in Portugal or anywhere, don't rely on a mortgage broker telling you he can get you a mortgage when signing a purchase agreement. Insist on a contingency clause no matter how sure the broker is about your loan.

A few years ago, looking to purchase a rental in Paris, we considered the idea of refinancing another apartment we own in that city. We knew that few banks were lending to nonresidents in France at the time, so we spoke with a mortgage broker. The broker sent our application to what turned out to be the only bank in France that would consider the kind of refinance we were looking for. She got a preliminary approval of our file. Fortunately, we knew that didn't guarantee anything and included a financing contingency clause in the purchase contract for the new property.

The bank requested information on the property we were buying, which we sent them. Then they asked for more financial information, which we provided. Then they went quiet. When we'd ask the broker for an update, she'd tell us that the bank was "working on the file." Eventually, we insisted on speaking with the bank directly. Mortgage brokers don't like to allow that. They worry you'll try to cut them out of the deal. We didn't want to bypass the broker, but we needed to understand what was going on. The purchase contract included a deadline for the mortgage approval. We had only so much time to back out of the deal without losing our down payment.

Finally, we were able to speak with the department head at the bank. As we suspected, they'd found something in our file that they didn't like—namely, that we were legal and fiscal residents of Panama. This was shortly after the Panama Papers scandal, and anything to do with the country was a red flag. It didn't matter that our tax returns and bank statements showed that we qualified for the loan. Our Panama connection blackballed us. The bank wasn't going to approve our loan. However, they also weren't going to say they weren't going to approve our loan. They were holding onto the file, hoping we'd eventually go away quietly. It's not an uncommon strategy. Banks don't want to upset a mortgage broker who brings them lots of business.

17 Where a Productive Land Investment (of Less Than $50,000) Can Deliver Regular Pension Checks for the Rest of Your Life

No matter how big (or small) your real estate investment portfolio, it should include agriculture. A productive land investment can generate regular cash returns while creating a legacy for future family generations. This kind of buy can equate to a do-it-yourself pension plan, delivering regular checks for the rest of your life, as returns from an agri-buy can stretch out over decades.

The challenge historically has been finding a turnkey opportunity to earn money from agriculture that didn't require an investment of a million dollars or more. Today you have good options that require no dirty work and that you can act on with $50,000 or less. The internal rate of return (IRR) can be as high as 17% or 18% per year.

Top Market for Agriculture #1: Panama

We own two properties in Panama that came planted with teak. One is in a professional tree farm, where the plantation manager employs engineers and other technical staff to monitor the trees, manage the thinning process (important with teak), control water levels, and so forth, and has the infrastructure in place to harvest and sell the trees when they reach maturity.

The other property is a piece of land where the owner planted teak to take advantage of tax incentives offered by the Panamanian government. He put the trees in the ground and then forgot them, never watering, never thinning. When we were considering the purchase, we asked the friend who owns the professional operation where we're invested to come take a look and estimate the value of the trees on the land we were looking to buy. They were 10 years old at the time, meaning, in theory, another 15 years to harvest. When our friend made the trip, he found some trees that had been cut for fence posts. He counted the rings and confirmed that the trees were about 10 years old, but, he told us, they were the circumferences of five-year-old trees at his plantation. That's the difference professional management, the proper terrain and soil, the most suitable climate, and the right amount of water can make. The location of this random piece of land we bought isn't the best for growing teak. That was okay for us, because the teak was a bonus. We were buying the property for its riverfront situation and had other ideas for generating a return from it.

When investing in timber or other agriculture, unless you're an agronomist, you need to work with an experienced farm manager, as we discuss in Part III. Alternatively, you can invest with developers who have designed their projects to allow small investors to take turnkey positions.

Panama has become a leader in this market niche, for teak and other trees for timber, fruit trees, and even cash crops. When shopping options, favor developers who choose to hold back portions of their plantations for their own harvests. This means they are investing for the long-term, alongside you, and that they believe in the potential of their crops. They are inviting you and other small investors to participate because that allows them to expand and realize economies of scale more quickly. You want to be sure, though, that they aren't simply raising money with no serious farming agenda.

Also favor investments that allow you to own the land. The process involved with segregating small pieces of agricultural land is lengthy and cumbersome, but some agricultural developers take it on. This means you are able to take title to the land where your trees or crops are planted and helps to mitigate overall risk. Worst case, if the harvests don't materialize as projected, you have the land to fall back on.

Top Market for Agriculture #2: Colombia

Our top choice for a timber investment beyond teak is Colombia, where you'll have to settle for buying shares of a reforestation company. In this country, the minimum segregation size for agricultural land is too big to allow developers to title lots small enough to be individual investor-friendly. If you have $1 million or more to invest, you could buy 1,000 hectares and hire a forestry company to plant and manage the trees and the harvests for you. If you don't, look for opportunities to invest $50,000 in shares of a timber plantation.

Top Market for Agriculture #3: Spain

In Europe, you won't find timber investment opportunities that come with land ownership—again because of the cost of segregating and transferring small parcels of land—but you can own the trees. Plantations in this part of the world are smaller than they can be in the Americas or Asia, typically fewer than 100 hectares, but that's enough to achieve some economies of scale.

Many countries where timber is a viable investment offer incentives, ranging from tax breaks to government grants. If you're buying in a development, these should pass on to you as an investor.

Top Tip from Lief

Investing in Agriculture Without the Land

One agriculture-related cash-flow opportunity that is beginning to attract significant attention isn't strictly real estate because it doesn't require land.

Hydroponic and aquaponic projects are being developed many places around the world where the land or weather isn't conducive to growing certain crops. You can put a greenhouse on infertile land or even on a rooftop and grow tomatoes or lettuce. It's an environmentally friendly approach to producing harvests, because these greenhouse systems use less water than land-based plantations and no pesticides or chemical fertilizers.

When investing in hydroponics, you're buying either an individual piece of equipment or a greenhouse containing equipment. The developer either owns or leases the land where the hydroponics hardware is placed, sources and builds the systems, then manages the farm production and sales.

V

How to Buy
Real Estate Overseas
in Eight Easy Steps

When we arrived in Waterford in 1998 and decided we wanted to own a home of our own there, we set out to find one the way any couple of Americans would set out to buy a house. We dropped by a real estate agent's office in the center of Waterford City. We sat down with Mr. O'Shea and gave him the rundown on the kind of house we were looking for. Georgian, stone, at least three bedrooms and three baths, with a bit of land for a garden, and maybe an old barn for a pony. Mr. O'Shea seemed to take our criteria under advisement and suggested a time later in the week when one of his agents could show us available properties.

That first day out, we saw four houses, not one of which in any way fit the description we'd given to Mr. O'Shea in his office. Instead, his agent kept taking us to see new-built "bungalows" in "estates," as the Irish refer to the suburban housing subdivisions that were popping up all across the country when we arrived on the scene. Kathleen refused to get out of the car to walk through the fourth place. It looked just like the three we'd already seen and that we'd already explained weren't anything like what we were interested in buying.

The Celtic Tiger was an established economic phenomenon by the time we took up residence in Waterford, and the better part of the money that boom was throwing off was being plowed into real estate—building it, buying it, selling it, one Irishman to another. Dozens of the housing estates of the kind Mr. O'Shea's team was so intent on introducing to us were being developed across the Emerald Isle in what was the start of what proved to be one of biggest Ponzi schemes in history. Over the next seven years that we lived in Ireland, the real estate market in this country continued up and up and up. It was a self-fueling spiral.

This chaotically expanding Irish marketplace of the late 1990s was our introduction to shopping for real estate in a foreign country. It took us months to begin to realize even how much we didn't know what we didn't know. We'd like to save you the frustration and the confusion that we suffered as we felt our way through that first purchase in Ireland and other early property buys. Here, therefore, is how you buy real estate overseas, in eight easy steps.

18

Do Your Research and Identify Three Destinations That Fit Your Budget and Your Lifestyle Goals

The first step is to decide where you're interested in investing. Don't chase promises of high yields in Bulgaria if you have no desire to be in Bulgaria. Even some places where we have enjoyed spending time, we've opted not to invest because we didn't expect to be able to return often or at all even if we owned property there. To maximize your return on a cash-flowing investment anywhere, you should plan to visit the property at least once a year.

Focus on destinations where you'd enjoy vacationing. In these pages, we target Portugal, Spain, Mexico, Colombia, Brazil, Panama, and the Dominican Republic, because those countries offer good investment opportunities in 2020 and will continue to do so long term. These aren't the only places you can find good real estate cash-flow investments overseas, but if one or more of those destinations appeals to you as a place to visit, then that's the place to start.

If you vacation internationally, think back over places that you'd like an excuse to return to, then look into the current local real estate opportunities.

If you like to dive, beach and diving destinations in the Caribbean should be at the top of your shopping list. If you're a fan of classic architecture and Old World history, look first in Europe. Sailors might look in locations with marinas. Surfers should prioritize countries in the Americas with a Pacific coast.

You get the idea.

Make a list of at least three destinations before planning your first scouting trip. Give yourself options for where to go. You could find that the place you are most excited about doesn't make sense for some reason.

In each location you visit, schedule time both to view properties and to have fun. Always remind yourself that buying a cash-flowing property overseas isn't only about the money. This is as much about reinventing your lifestyle as it is about building a portfolio. Plan out your visit but leave yourself time to wander around. Walking is the best way to get a feel for a place, and we prioritize this when scouting a new destination. We want to develop a baseline lay of the land before meeting with a real estate agent.

Also allow time for meetings with a real estate attorney and maybe a bank on that first trip.

In most markets where you'll be interested in shopping, you'll find that real estate agents will resist scheduling viewings until you're in the country. If they've worked with foreigners in the past, they've been burned by people changing their plans and not showing up without warning. In some tourist markets, real estate agents who've wasted time with looky-loos killing time on vacation might ask you to pay a fee for them to show you around. Respect the real estate agent's time.

Real estate attorneys on the other hand should be willing to schedule an appointment before you get on a plane as long as you have a solid date for when you'll be in the country. If you don't have a lead for a good real estate attorney before you arrive, ask the real estate agents you're speaking with for a recommendation. You can also check the U.S. Embassy website for that country, which should include a list of English-speaking attorneys by specialty. Interview at least two attorneys.

Before you get on the plane, do as much research online as you can to get an idea of property prices. We Americans are used to being able to search for comps on websites like Zillow. No such services exist in most markets outside North America, because almost nowhere else in the world operates with a multiple listing service. Where you find a multiple listing service in place, they aren't helpful. To get an idea what's available in a market, you'll have to speak with several real estate agents and see a range of properties. Agents don't cooperate, so it's not disloyal for you, as the buyer, to work with several different ones. It's the only way to get a proper overview of the market. We found that out the hard way in Ireland.

While the Internet is a good place to start looking, any foreign property listings you find searching online in English are going to be priced at a premium. To break through the gringo-pricing barrier, you'll need to do some research online in the local language. With online translators, it's easy these days.

Another important connection to make during any initial scouting trip is with a rental management company. The rental manager is key to success with a cash-flow investment anywhere. Some real estate agencies offer rental management services. Depending on the market, this can be the best option. Before committing, though, research the availability of independent management.

Finally, when scouting a new market and even when returning to a market where you have experience, try to speak with other foreign property owners and investors. We're not talking about the geezer in the corner of the local bar who knows everyone and everything. He's usually a time sucker who likes to hear himself talk. Make an effort to connect with serious people with firsthand experience in the market. Your real estate agent and attorney probably have clients they could introduce you to, and social media makes it easy to connect with like-minded people anywhere on the planet.

19 Figure Your Budget, Including the Round-trip Costs of Buying and Selling

When we bought our first property overseas, in Ireland, we were thinking only about the purchase price and the down payment required, given the financing we believed we'd qualify for. That's how we set our budget as we started our search. We didn't speak with a real estate attorney until after we'd begun looking at houses. Fortunately, we had the conversation before we settled on a specific property.

Transaction costs when buying a piece of real estate in the United States are nominal and related mostly to financing. In Chicago, for example, the buyer pays a transfer tax, but, at 0.75%, it's nominal. Lief doesn't remember it and figures it must have been rolled into the rest of the closing costs and buried in the title company disclosure information.

In Ireland, however, as well as in most of the 25 countries where we've bought real estate, the buyer pays a government transfer tax that isn't nominal. When we bought in Ireland, the transfer tax was 9%. That meant that the money we had available for a down payment was less than we had calculated. We had to back out that unexpected 9%.

At the time we resigned ourselves to the transfer tax by reminding ourselves that Ireland doesn't charge property tax. Hold a property for four or five years, and the total cost of your property would be comparable to your total cost in the United States including property tax. Hold longer, and you came out ahead.

Transfer taxes, charged in many countries, range from 1% to 10%. Governments can use them to help dampen a frothy real estate market. That's why the rate in Ireland was 9% when we bought in 1999. Today, Ireland's transfer tax, or stamp duty, as it is called in commonwealth countries, is 1% up to 1 million euros of value and 2% for any amount over 1 million euros.

A true transfer tax isn't recoverable. However, some countries, including Nicaragua, for example, charge the seller a tax at the time of closing that is sometimes referred to as a transfer tax but that is really a capital gains withholding tax. Although this fee is charged to the seller, he typically passes it on to the buyer. When charged, this fee is a way for the country to make sure it gets paid at least some of the income tax due on the capital gains from the eventual resale of a piece of property. Governments of countries with active foreign property markets understand that most foreign buyers aren't going to file tax returns when selling a real estate holding in that country. The tax charged at the point of sale is meant to bring any eventual tax owed on any eventual capital gain forward. If by some chance the withholding tax is more than what the capital gains tax would be (usually it won't be), you can then file a tax return to try to get a refund of the difference.

Thanks to transfer taxes, buying and flipping for a quick profit is not common in most overseas markets. While you can buy a piece of real estate in the United States with a high loan-to-value (LTV) mortgage, do some work, then turn around and sell the property for, say, a 10% profit on your purchase price that equates to a 100% profit on your 5% down payment after paying the real estate agent, that's not a viable strategy most places overseas. Especially as high LTV financing isn't easy to get as a foreigner.

Another upfront cost to ask about is agent commissions. In most countries, as in the United States and Canada, the list price includes the sales commission, meaning the commission comes out of the seller's end. However, in some countries, including Argentina and Italy, for example, the buyer and the seller split the agent commission. If this is the case in the market where you're buying, you need to factor this additional cost into your budget.

In some markets, the commission isn't included in the listing price but added on top, increasing your purchase price. This can be the case in France, though the strategy is less common today than in the past and must be disclosed in the listing advertisement.

Attorney and notary costs should run 0.5% to 1% of the transaction cost, with the percentage decreasing as the value of the transaction increases. Unfortunately, in some Latin American countries, some attorneys notice how much real estate agents make from property transactions and get the idea that they should make more. The result is that attorney fees in this part of the world can be all over the board. Confirm the fee for a particular transaction with your attorney before you begin to process any paperwork with him. Don't assume that his rates will be comparable to rates quoted you by another attorney.

Note that, unlike a notary in the United States, a notary in a civil law country is a licensed attorney with an additional license (specific for performing the duties of a notary) or title granted by the government. These are semigovernmental agents who act as gatekeepers for official documents, including property titles. In France, for example, your *notaire* manages the entire real estate purchase process (meaning you don't need a regular attorney; your *notaire* takes the place of an attorney), including the title check and the transfer of title. In other countries, the notary is simply the official registration agent.

Registration fees should amount to less than 0.5% of the purchase price but are typically charged as a set fee, rather than as a percentage of the purchase price.

Understanding your total closing costs when buying is important to your budget planning. This is another reason to use a real estate attorney. He can help confirm your costs. Your real estate agent should be able to help, too, and, if you're buying in a market where foreign buyers are common, he might have a buyer information sheet to share with you, detailing all costs a buyer is liable for.

Once you've determined your costs on the buy side, detail the costs for when you sell. This will give you the round-trip costs of your purchase.

Whereas the possibility of a transfer tax might give you pause as you research potential overseas investment markets, you'll be glad to hear that sales commission rates in many countries are well below the 5% to 6% standard in the United States and Canada. The real estate agent's fee in Colombia is only 3%. In fact, the upfront closing costs in Colombia are low, as well, making it one of the lowest round-trip cost destinations you'll find. The total cost of buying and then selling in this country is 5.25% to 6.5%.

On the high side is Andorra. While you're not likely to buy an investment property in high-rent Andorra, it's worth noting that the round-trip costs in this country range from 12% to 17.5%. Why such a wide range? Agents charge from 5% to as much 10%, depending on the agency and the price and location of the property.

Other countries where real estate agent fees are notably high include Belize and the Bay Islands of Honduras, where the standard agent's commission is 10%.

Another cost to understand before you buy in any market is the country's capital gains tax. Americans are liable for capital gains tax in the United States on any profits when selling property overseas, but you get a tax credit for whatever capital gains tax is paid in the country where the property is located. If the tax owed is greater in the foreign country than in the United States, you owe nothing on the U.S. side. If the tax owed in the foreign market is lower than the U.S. tax, you pay the difference on the U.S. side. Speak with your U.S. tax preparer for details on how these foreign tax credits work.

Not all countries charge capital gains tax on real estate profits. Rental property owned in New Zealand for five years or more is not liable for capital gains tax. In France, the capital gains tax on real estate is reduced for nonresidents by 6% a year starting with the sixth year of ownership. Own for 22 years or longer, and you owe no capital gains taxes. It's France, though, so that's not the end of the story. You're also liable for a social charge on the gain that is reduced every year after the fifth year of ownership and reaches 0 after 30 years. Sell before five years, and you'll be liable for 19% capital gains tax and 7.5% in social charges.

Of course, Americans owe capital gains taxes in the United States even if no capital gains tax is charged in the foreign country. And remember that things like capital gains tax rates change, as has happened in Colombia since we bought there. When we made our investment, capital gains were taxed at the highest income tax band. The country has since instituted a separate capital gains tax rate of 10%.

We detail the round-trip costs for 20 key markets in Appendix A.

20 Build an In-country Network of Reliable Contacts

Over the course of our multidecade overseas real estate investing careers, we have met hundreds if not thousands of real estate agents and developers, real estate attorneys, accountants, local investors, expat investors, and rental property managers. Most we never did business with, some we've remained in touch with, and a handful of them have become friends and even partners in different real estate investments. You're welcome to tap into our network to get yourself started. At our website (www.liveandinvestoverseas.com) you'll find, as the name suggests, resources for both living and investing overseas, including several free e-letters, one dedicated to buying and owning overseas property(www.overseaspropertyalert.com).

You'll also want to build your own personal network. The key contacts are a real estate agent, a real estate attorney, and a rental management company (or person). In fact, ideally, you want more than one of each in each market where you're focused or active. Also speak with other property owners in the markets where you're shopping, both expats and locals, who might give you very different perspectives on the market. Meet with at least one banker, both because you'll need to open a bank account should you buy in that country and also because a banker can have different market insights to share.

Taxi drivers are other good sources of economic and market context. They talk to people all day long, and they are living the local life. Not that you're going to base your buy decision on the advice of a cab driver, but add their insights to your knowledge base.

If you don't speak the local language, you'll need either to restrict yourself to English-speaking resources or to engage a translator. We have always chosen to work with English-speaking real estate agents and attorneys in the countries where we've invested. We both speak Spanish well enough to work with Spanish-speaking contacts, and sometimes we do in the interest of gaining better background. However, when we're ready to act, we prefer to work with professionals who have experience with foreigners. We foreign buyers operate differently than local buyers, so we seek out agents and attorneys who've helped others like us invest successfully.

That said, we've learned not to become instantly comfortable with or to trust a real estate agent solely because he speaks English.

Years ago, Lief was presenting the idea of buying property overseas at a conference. He explained that many of the gringo (North American) real estate agents you can run into in Central America in particular may not have been in the country very long and may not have had any real estate experience before they landed. Lief made up a story on the spot to explain. "Maybe your real estate agent on Roatan you're speaking with doesn't know that market at all yet. He could have just moved from Florida three months ago where he was a travel agent," he said.

As he gave the hypothetical example, someone at the back of the room got up and stormed out. After his presentation, the conference director came up to Lief to tell him he had to apologize. "For what?" Lief asked. "I've been on stage. How could I have insulted someone while up on stage?"

It turns out one of the agents participating in the event who was with a real estate agency from Roatan had only been with the agency for three months. In fact, had only moved to Roatan three months before from Florida … where he had been a travel agent.

Although Lief really did make up the example on the spot, it was based on long experience dealing with real estate agents in markets across Central and Latin America. North Americans retire or otherwise move to their dream destinations overseas and either get bored or need to earn money. Becoming a real estate agent is the easiest job to get. In some cases, the only job they can take because they don't have work permits, and no training or licensing is required.

If the real estate agent you're speaking with isn't local, ask them how long they've been in the country. Ask them how long they've been selling real estate. If they've been in the country less than a year but have real estate experience from where they came from, then they're likely to have educated themselves quickly on the current state of the local market. You're better off working with that guy than with a former travel agent fresh off the boat from Florida.

You should ask the same question of a local trying to sell you real estate. How long have they been in the business? You'll find that everyone you meet anywhere in Latin America will have a piece of real estate to sell you. Mention to your taxi driver that you're shopping for an apartment, and he'll know someone who has one for sale. That can be an effective strategy for searching at a local level, but you need a lot of experience and knowledge of the local market before making yourself vulnerable in this way.

When shopping in the United States, you entertain any conversation about the purchase of a piece of real estate taking many things for granted. You're confident not only that you don't have to worry about things like history of ownership and promised future amenities, but also that, should something go wrong, you'll have some recourse. You assume that you could file your grievance with some oversight agency. Worst case, there'll always be somebody you could sue—right?

There's no Honduran government agency that regulates the sale of real estate to foreign buyers, and how are you going to sue somebody in Nicaragua? You aren't. So you need to make sure you don't end up in a situation where that seems your only option. How do you do that? As we're explaining, you engage a good attorney to protect your interests.

Your attorney is your most important ally when buying, selling, or renting real estate in any overseas market. While you might buy real estate in the United States without ever thinking of engaging an attorney, we suggest that you never buy real estate in another country without—first thing, before you do anything else—finding a local attorney you can trust who speaks real English, who has experience working with foreigners, and, who, critically, works for you. Not for the seller, not for the property developer, but for you, and sharing doesn't count. If you're sharing an attorney with the developer or seller, whose interests come first in his mind when an issue arises? Note that this is what most developers in most developing markets push for. "My attorney's great," the developer you're intending to buy from will tell you. "He has helped dozens of Americans buy here. He knows his stuff. You'll love him. I'll put you in touch."

Resist the temptation. It will seem the easy, efficient solution, but it puts you at a disadvantage throughout the purchase process.

That's the first important point to understand about engaging an attorney to represent your interests as you shop for real estate in any foreign market. The second has to do with language. What do we mean when we say you need an attorney who speaks "real" English? We mean that you need to find an attorney who understands what you say when you speak to him not only literally but figuratively, as well. Think of the differences between U.S. English, British English, and Aussie English and the misunderstandings that can occur as a result. Now imagine you're speaking to someone who learned his English with the help of a tutor later in life or someone who learned to speak English by watching MTV as a kid (I've known many in many places around the world for whom this has been the case). That person may understand the words you're speaking, but that doesn't mean he's following your underlying meanings, your slang, your metaphors, your points of reference, and so forth. When your money is on the table, you want someone who processes the nuances of your instructions as well as the literal details.

Finding a good local attorney, one who speaks English and who has had experience with foreign property buyers, should be your number-one priority when you enter a new market with the intent to buy—your first order of business—best accomplished before you begin scouting, searching, or viewing. How do you find a good attorney in a foreign country? You do it by referral. You don't want to make this decision based on an Internet search. You want to work with an attorney you find via some personal recommendation, ideally the personal recommendation of a fellow expat. Ask everyone you communicate with in any market where you're thinking about buying for an attorney reference. Identify two or three attorneys whose names come up again and again. Contact them. Interview them, by e-mail and then by phone. Take time to get to know them.

Once you've made this all-important first connection, you can build out your in-country network of contacts from there. The attorney you choose to work with can recommend real estate agents, bankers, accountants, even carpenters, contractors, electricians, and, very important, other expats who've already invested in the country. This is how we've built networks of contacts that we trust and that in some cases I've now worked with for going on three decades in dozens of countries.

In addition, when trying to get your head around a new market, seek out and spend time with locals not in the real estate business, from taxi drivers to waitresses, shop owners to bar tenders. Their insights into the real estate market can be most valuable. In Medellín, for example, on one of our first scouting trips, we had one of our most helpful conversations with an antiques dealer whose shop we stopped in one Saturday afternoon. Smart, successful local businesspeople can give you valuable insights into a market that a real estate agent might neglect to mention.

Ask everyone you speak with the same questions. You'll be surprised by the variety of answers you'll get. Some will be completely contradictory. In some cases, you might ask six people the same question and get six different responses. Our first scouting trip in Medellín, we asked one real estate agent we met with if it were possible for a foreigner to open a bank account in Colombia. "Yes, of course, no problem. You just need your passport," he told us. We asked another real estate agent we met with the same question. "To open a bank account in Colombia, a foreigner needs a *cedula*. Do you know what that is?" he asked. Yes, we knew what that was—a residency card issued only to those with legal foreign residence status. That left us out.

Here's a checklist of questions you should also ask everyone you encounter in any new market you enter:

- Which are considered the "nicest" neighborhoods?
- Which are considered the up-and-coming neighborhoods?
- How much does an apartment or a house cost? Boil this down to a per-square-meter price so you can compare among areas within the country and among other countries.
- Where are most foreigners buying? Why?
- What types of properties are most foreigners buying (one-bedroom apartments, houses, undeveloped land, etc.)? Why?
- Are most foreigners buying for personal use or for investment?
- Is there an active rentals market? Short-term, long-term, or both?
- How much would a particular property rent for per month long-term or per week short-term?
- Where would you (speaking to a real estate agent, an attorney, a business owner, an expat, or a taxi driver) invest yourself right now? Why?
- In which direction is the market moving?

Ask general questions about the local economy and local industry. Ask about the current president or whoever is in charge of running things. Not to be political but to get a read on the political situation from the man on the street. Ask about taxes. Are they high? Do people pay them? How are they collected? Is there a property tax? On what value is it based? Again, you'll be amazed at the variety of answers you'll receive. All this input, conflicting though it will seem, will help give you the lay of the land. The more conflicting the responses, the wilder the market.

The next step is to begin to get a handle on procedures. For this, you'll need help from your attorney. Here's a checklist of questions to ask him:

- What are the transaction costs for buying and selling real estate? You'll want to know the "round-trip" costs, as we refer to them, for a single piece of property. In some markets, it is more expensive to buy than to sell and vice versa. You don't want to find out too late that, while it cost only 2% to get into an investment, it's going to cost you 15% to get out.
- What is the buying process? What documents are required? What is a typical down payment? Are there any local nuances you should know? In many emerging markets, for example, you'll be told that it's common practice for the purchase price for a piece of real estate to be understated (perhaps significantly) on the sales documents. This can have advantages (when it comes to paying property taxes, for example), but it also can create problems down the road, to do with capital gains tax and foreign exchange controls if they exist. Even if you're assured that "everyone does it," we recommend that you don't. Even if it means paying the seller a little more (as it can), insist that the full purchase price be represented on the purchase documents.

Exchange controls are an important point to understand with the help of your attorney. Will you have any trouble taking your money back out of the country when you decide you're ready to do so?

While you're playing private detective and asking everyone you meet the same series of questions, you also want to be observing. As you are learning your way around the area, do you notice signs of an active economy? Are people out at the malls and restaurants shopping, spending? What's the infrastructure like? Are the roads well maintained? Are the parks and public areas taken care of? Do you see garbage in the streets or on the sidewalks?

A strong local economy can translate into one possible exit strategy for your real estate purchase. If no local economy exists or if the local economy is small and limited, then you're likely going to be limited to selling to another foreigner when the time comes for you to cash out. This is the case in many resort markets in Mexico and Spain, for example. Having a local market can reduce your investment risk.

Your first visit to any new market, see as many properties in as many different neighborhoods and areas as you have time for. You want to get a feel for the type of construction, the options for building materials, common amenities, and so forth. See how apartments are typically laid out. Is space well used? Collect and catalogue every listing sheet for every property you view.

Then go home. Don't buy anything your first trip no matter how tempted you are. Take all your boots-on-the-ground information with you back wherever you came from. Sift through it. Compare responses. Fact-check what you can with as many sources as possible.

An in-country network of reliable contacts is the first part of the pre-purchase infrastructure you need to create. The second part has to do with logistics. Here's a checklist for the administrative infrastructure you're going to need in any country where you purchase real estate:

- A local bank account or whatever alternative is going to allow you to transfer money into the country and then pay local expenses. In Colombia, for example, you'll have trouble opening a bank account as a nonresident foreigner. It'll be much easier (and just as effective) to open what's called a "fiduciary" account. This is the equivalent of a Schwab account in the United States.

- The ability to wire funds from your home-base bank account using fax or phone instructions. This may mean switching banks at home, because some US banks require you to come to your bank branch in person to organize a wire transfer. This won't work if you happen to be in Belize, say, or Italy at the time you decide you need to send the wire.

- The holding structure for the property if you aren't going to take title in your own name—a real estate holding company or a limited liability company (LLC), for example (more on this in Chapter 24).

- A bank account for that company. We recommend you start the process to open this account as soon as the company is set up, even if you don't intend to use it for some time. It's increasingly difficult to open a bank account anywhere in the world as a nonresident, and it's more difficult still to open a nonresident corporate account.

When you have an in-country network of support established and the necessary purchase infrastructure in place, you're ready for the next step—finding the piece of property you want to buy.

21 Identify a Purchase

Before you begin looking at properties for potential investment, we recommend creating a spreadsheet to track the details for each rental you view. This will make it much easier for you to compare each option against all the others. When shopping in Latin American markets, don't expect listing sheets. Sometimes you'll be lucky if the agent showing you the apartment is able to answer your questions even about basic things like total square meters and building fees.

What data should you record for each property you view? Your spreadsheet should include the price, the total size in square meters (so you can compare property prices by square meter; this is the only way to get an apples-to-apples read on relative costs), monthly HOA fees, estimated monthly utility expenses, property taxes, and, if they property is currently operating as a rental, occupancy rates over the past two years and the average rent. If the property doesn't have rental history, estimate occupancy and gross rental income with help from the real estate agent and rental managers you interview. Then use the occupancy rates, rental figures, and sales price to calculate net rental yield. This net rental yield projection is a key factor in making a buy decision.

If you haven't ever created a spreadsheet to calculate net yields on a rental property, you can download one to get you started at our Live and Invest Overseas website, liveandinvestoverseas .com/howtodooverseascashflowmath. In some cases, you'll be able to get a good idea of the projected net rental yield in advance of a viewing. If your estimated net yield is less than 5%, you might want to skip seeing that particular property. On the other hand, the more properties you see the better you become at sizing up one opportunity versus another. Plus, the more time spent with your real estate agent, the better you're able to judge his competence and experience.

Unless you're buying largely for personal use and know without question where you want to purchase, the biggest challenge of buying property overseas can be identifying where to buy. How do you move from the very general notion that you'd like to own cash-flowing real estate overseas to identifying where and what, specifically, to buy?

It takes time and what we refer to as "being in the market." When you target a country or a region as a place where you think you want to invest, you need then to work to position yourself so that you're ready to act when the right opportunity presents itself. You do this by researching, scouting, and staying connected. This is where the in-country network of support you've built, starting with a local attorney you trust, begins to pay off. When you've identified a big-picture location for purchase, make everyone you know in that location aware that you're in the market, looking for an opportunity. Give them an idea of what kind of property you're shopping for (size, specific location, intended use) and your budget.

You can't wake up one morning and decide you're going to invest in a rental property in Panama, a Caribbean beach house in Belize, or an apartment in Paris. Well, you could, and you could then proceed quickly to buy. But, operating that way, the chances that you'll get the best deal possible are slim and the chances that things won't play out the way you hope are not.

You need to be "in a market" long enough to understand the difference between the local market and the gringo one. You need the experience of vetting opportunities and of communicating with sellers. You need to determine your own idea of comparables and of what a piece of property of the description you're looking to buy "should" cost. You aren't going to accomplish those things in a single visit to a country or after a few weeks of Internet research. To buy right, you need to give the in-country contacts and resources you've developed a chance to connect you in real time. You need to leverage their boots on the ground, because, unless you're taking up temporary residence in the place yourself while conducting your property search (not a bad idea but usually not possible), you don't have boots on the ground of your own.

Colombia, for example, was a new market for us when we decided we wanted to invest in a property in Medellín. Even though we'd bought real estate in many other foreign countries many times before, we moved slowly. We solicited a local attorney recommendation from an expat friend who had recently bought in Medellín himself. We traveled to Medellín to meet the attorney in person, then, with his help, we developed a network of connections, including three real estate agents (one gringo, two local), a banker, and a contractor (as we knew we would be shopping for a renovation project). We returned to the country five times over 10 months, each time expanding our network and furthering our education. Finally, after nearly a year of focused effort and after viewing dozens of apartments for sale, we made a choice and an offer. A year is possibly excessive. We've purchased in other new markets after six months of attention or less. Our point is that, even if you've got years of experience at this, it takes time to identify a purchase, especially if you're targeting what for you is a new market.

One way to narrow your search for a rental property is to ask the rental managers you meet with what rents best in that market and if any specific type of rental is currently in short supply. This is the approach we took when shopping for our first rental in Paris.

The short-term rental industry is well established in Paris. It was a strong and growing industry decades before Airbnb. Foreigners buy pieds-a-terre to stay in when they visit Paris and rent out when they aren't there. Most of these buyers don't have big budgets; these are second homes in one of the world's most expensive property markets. The apartments they buy tend to be small—studios and small one-bedrooms. Thus, that's the majority of the short-tern rental inventory available in Paris.

The rental manager we met with in advance of beginning the search for our first rental property in Paris made the point that what she could really use was a two- or even a three-bedroom apartment. The demand for bigger rentals is much smaller than the demand for studios and one-bedrooms, but it's seriously underserviced. Two couples traveling together could rent two one-bedroom apartments near to each other, but a family didn't have a good option. Meantime, a single couple wouldn't be opposed to renting a two-bedroom apartment if the price and location were right, even if they didn't need the second bedroom. In other words, a two-bedroom apartment allowed more flexibility than a smaller place.

In addition to insights and recommendations about what size and configuration (studio, one bedroom, two bedroom, etc.) could be more or less rentable, a rental manager should be able to give you ideas regarding the best neighborhoods, important apartment amenities, and nearby services that renters are looking for in that market.

Now that you know what you're looking for, you can pass your parameters on to the real estate agents you've contacted.

Use every property you see as a learning experience even if it doesn't meet your parameters, but don't spend much time in a place you know you're not going to buy. Move on quickly to the next one, all the while keeping notes to enter into your tracking spreadsheet when you get back to your computer.

You'll want to see enough properties to feel confident in your buy decision when you make it. At the same time, you don't need to see every property on the market. One friend who has bought rentals in at least a half-dozen countries has been known to end up with more than 100 entries in his spreadsheet when looking at a new market. He's retired so he has that kind of time. He's also a former engineer. He likes data.

The problem with collecting that much data is that you can lose sight of the goal—which is to buy a property that makes good cash flow sense and that also serves your personal lifestyle agendas. Not everything about this can be calculated in a spreadsheet. You don't need to analyze 100 properties down to the third decimal point in the projected yield. You need to get a good feel for the market, feel comfortable you're paying a good price, be confident in your net rental yield projection, and like the place. That last point—actually liking the property you decide to buy—is as important as all the others.

22 Negotiate the Purchase

The actual real estate purchase process varies by country, but, generally speaking, there are three steps:

First: Make an offer.
Second: Sign a sales agreement.
Third: Sign a sales contract.

It might seem that the sales agreement and the sales contract should be the same thing, but, in most countries, they aren't. In most of the world, the first one is not a purchase agreement but a "promise" to sell; the second one is the closing document that results in the property being titled in the new owner's name. Specifically, here's how this typically works:

You make an offer. Most offers are made in person or by telephone, either directly from the buyer to the seller or through a real estate agent. Offers are not typically conveyed in writing. Depending on the market, your offer can be a starting point for a price negotiation. You should seek some advice in advance from others with experience in the market as to what's culturally acceptable on this front. Should you make a lowball offer with the intention of meeting the seller midway between that number and the asking price? Should you offer 10% less than is being asked? Should you expect a counteroffer? If the seller accepts your offer, are you bound to follow through, if not by law perhaps by local custom? And so forth …

You execute a sales agreement (*promesa de compraventa* in Spanish or *compromise de vente* in French). This can be an optional step depending on the country and whether you're ready to move to the closing right away. The *promesa* is a binding contract that outlines the terms of the sale to come. It's similar in function to a real estate sales contract in the United States and includes details for the down payment (including under what conditions it is refundable), spells out terms for full payment, sets a closing date, and specifies penalties for default. If you're buying in a country where it's possible and where you're planning to obtain local bank financing for the purchase (in many

European countries, for example), your sales agreement should also contain a condition stating that, if your application for a mortgage is not successful, your deposit will be refunded.

Include any contingency even if you can't imagine you're going to need it. A friend was in the market for an apartment in Portugal that he'd use part of the year himself and rent out otherwise. He needed bank financing and met with a local mortgage broker. He filled out an application, which the broker submitted to several banks. The broker reported to our friend that he'd been preapproved for a mortgage. On the strength of that preapproval, our friend went shopping.

When he found the apartment he wanted to buy, our friend asked the bank for final confirmation of the loan. The bank declined because our friend couldn't provide acceptable proof of income. He was retired. All his income came from passive investments. He could show brokerage statements. He could show income history for rental properties. But the bank wanted a certified tax return from an accountant and had assumed this would be forthcoming when pre-approving the loan.

Our friend couldn't find an accountant willing to sign such a statement, because, again, he didn't have any verifiable earned income.

Because he'd gotten the preapproval from the bank and assurances from the mortgage broker that the loan would go through, our friend hadn't included a mortgage contingency in the purchase agreement. He was unable to close on the purchase and lost his 10% deposit.

Note that, in France, you have a seven-day "cooling off" period from the date you sign the *compromise de vente*, during which time you can withdraw from the sale without penalty but the seller cannot. A word of caution: We know a couple who bought a home and then decided, during the cooling-off period, that they had made a mistake. They tried to contact the *notaire* and then the agent on the seventh day only to find that it was a national holiday in France and both the attorney's and the agent's offices were closed. The sale went through. Moral of the story: Make sure your *notaire* will be available during your cooling-off period.

You complete the closing documents (*escritura de compraventa* in Spanish *or acte de vente* in French). The *escritura* (or *acte de vente*, etc.) is the final document and serves as the deed to the property once it's been recorded in the local property registry. Until this document is registered, the title is still in the name of previous owner. Your notary generally should record the new *escritura* the day you sign it, though, sometimes, depending on the country, this document might not be recorded until a few days later.

In some extreme cases (Croatia is an example), it can be that the sales agreement is recorded (blocking any other sale of the property by the previous owner) while the government processes their paperwork to approve you as a foreign buyer. When we bought our farmhouse in Croatia, the actual title wasn't registered until more than a year after we'd paid for the property. Meantime, again, the executed sales agreement was recorded to protect us against the previous owner selling the place, which we'd already bought, from under us.

Your attorney or *notaire* will manage the purchase process for you, but you want to understand at least the big picture of what's going on and what you should expect to be happening each step along the way. If you don't speak the local language, your attorney should provide a translation of all the documents you'll need to sign. Note, though, that, everywhere in the world, a contract must be signed and registered in the local language to be legally valid.

The timing of each step becomes important if you're not living in the country. You don't want to book a flight to wherever you're buying for the closing of your purchase only to have the closing delayed. If you don't plan to return to the country for the closing, then you should obtain a power of attorney in that country before you leave, because it is always easier to do this locally than long distance. Depending on the country, you may need to have the power of attorney notarized (by the embassy of the country where you're buying) or apostilled. Obtaining an apostille requires a trip to your state's Secretary of State's office (or other similar national government office if you're not in the United States).

A typical down payment in most of the world is 10%, though, depending on what you're buying and where, you may have to put down as much as 40%. In the case of the apartment we purchased in Medellín, for example, the seller wanted 30% down because we were foreign buyers. We understood his concerns and agreed.

The down payment is typically made at the time you sign the sale agreement.

The period between the signing of the *promesa* and the signing of the *escritura* (that is, between the sale agreement and the closing) is your chance to carry out your final due diligence. You'll want to have vetted the purchase in advance of signing the sale agreement, first, because this is a binding document and, second, because the length of time and/or the limits on the conditions you can include in the sale agreement typically do not allow for complete due diligence.

Some countries (Panama, for example) have computerized central property registries making it easy for any attorney to check on the history of ownership for any property in the country. All that's needed is the property's registry number. Other places, where there is no such centralized property registry (Nicaragua), your attorney will have to go to the local mayor's office to check the title registry locally and in person.

This is a general overview of the property purchase process anywhere in the world. More specifically, this is how it works in most of Europe and in most of Latin America. However, if and when you eventually decide to purchase a home in another country, ask your real estate attorney for a complete outline of the local purchase process. He should have this in writing in English. If he doesn't, you should think about finding another attorney (one who is more experienced working with foreign buyers).

23 Close the Deal

Around the enormous table sat five adult siblings, three with spouses, two with attorneys, one with a grown son, plus the real estate agent for the seller, his two representatives, our real estate agent, our agent's boss, and Lief. It was the summer of 2003 in Buenos Aires. Over the preceding 12 months, we had bought three apartments in this city in the wake of Argentina's 2001 currency debacle and subsequent property crash. We arranged our schedules to be able to participate in the closing of the third apartment personally. We were purchasing from the five children of the elderly owner who had, not too long before, died in the apartment in question.

Argentines traditionally (with good reason) don't trust banks. Following the 2001 collapse, they really didn't trust banks. Real estate closings, therefore, were all-cash transactions that take place in the offices of currency houses, like the one where Lief sat that sunny summer morning. Papers went back and forth among siblings and attorneys, attorneys and agents, attorneys and attorneys. Then the agent for the currency house appeared. She had the cash. We had wired down our funds a couple of days beforehand so that the required cash bundles could be prepared. It was a $220,000 transaction.

The cash wasn't simply going from buyer (us) to seller. There were multiple sellers, each due a different percentage of the purchase amount. Into the room next, therefore, came the bill counter, the kind of machine that drug dealers and casinos might employ. Sister A got $22,000. Sister B got $35,000. Big brother who had been living in the house with his mother until she died got more than $100,000. The agent in charge passed him a plastic-wrapped brick of $100 bills and some "change" in the form of smaller individual packages.

Each sibling had his or her own ideas about how best to transport his or her cash. Sister A stuffed much of it inside her bra. One brother had a money belt for his relatively small take. The other sister gave some to her husband, put some in her purse, and gave some to her son. The brother who got the brick of 100s had little option but to use a small duffle bag.

The real estate agents took their commissions, and the attorneys took their fees and the amount required to register the title, again, all in cash. After everyone had claimed what was due him, a small pile remained in the middle of the table, a few thousand dollars left over that belonged to the buyers (us). Lief walked out with around $3,000 in cash in his jacket pocket, wondering if some local gang had figured out when real estate closings were being transacted at these currency houses so they could post someone at the entrances of the buildings and mug people as they walked out on to the street. (None of us was robbed.) The entire transaction took about an hour, with most of the time spent counting out bills.

Most closings aren't this dramatic, although it's not uncommon for *campesinos* in Central America (country folk in this part of the world) to request all cash at closing. One guy we purchased land from in Panama years ago supposedly transported his money back to his shack of a house in the middle of nowhere in a black garbage bag. He didn't have a bank account (and probably didn't trust banks anyway).

The particulars of closing on a real estate transaction vary by country, but more typical than all-cash is a cashier's check and a few signatures in front of a notary. You can avoid the entire process if you'd prefer, usually, by assigning your attorney a power of attorney, allowing him to sign the closing documents and manage the closing on your behalf. I'd suggest, though, being on hand in person at least for your first one or two closings and certainly if you buy in Argentina, just for the experience.

Even if you intend to be on hand yourself for a closing, we recommend that you process the paperwork to assign your attorney your power of attorney in advance anyway. Things happen. If for some reason at the last minute you're unable to make the trip to sign the closing documents yourself, having the power of attorney in place as a backup could save you from not being able to register the title in your name because of missing signatures or, even, from losing the purchase (and your deposit) altogether.

If you're getting a mortgage for the purchase, you may need to give your attorney a separate power of attorney allowing him to sign the mortgage documents (though sometimes you can sign these in advance of the official closing). Confirm with your bank what you need to have in place to ensure that this part of the closing goes smoothly.

Key, of course, to any property closing is the payment. Some of it could be via a mortgage, but, for any purchase, at least part of the payment will be in cash, requiring you to get cash where it needs to be when it needs to be there. We discuss the challenges and considerations associated with accomplishing this in detail in Part VIII.

24 Take Title

If you purchase a piece of real estate in another country, should you have the ownership documents issued in your name or, perhaps, in the name of a corporation? If a corporation, should it be a local company (formed in the jurisdiction where you're purchasing) or one based somewhere else?

To make the right choice for how to hold the title for a piece of foreign property you intend to purchase, you should consider two things: taxes and your estate.

Understand the tax obligations both in the country where you're buying and also in the United States if you're an American. Likewise, implications for your estate should be considered both locally and back home.

Let's take Panama as an example. The typical way to hold real estate in this country is through a Panamanian corporation. This provides a positive tax effect in Panama whenever you resell, because you're not, in fact, selling the piece of property but the company that owns it. This minimizes the capital gains tax. On the other hand, owning a piece of property in a Panamanian corporation can create a negative U.S. tax effect for an American. Specifically, this can result in the gains being taxed at income rather than at capital-gains rates. You have to weigh the potential liabilities.

Regarding the estate issue, you need to make sure you understand both inheritance laws and estate taxes in the country where you're buying. Here, let's take France as an example. The inheritance laws in this country may surprise you and certainly can result in your property ending up somewhere other than where you'd like it to go following your death unless you have a will that the French will recognize. Particular issues arise if you are in a second marriage, for example, or have stepchildren to whom you'd like to leave some ownership of some French asset. Die without a will valid in France, and this is not what will happen. The default French inheritance distribution follows blood. Without proper planning, your assets could end up going to your uncle (or some other random relative) rather than to the people you'd like to have them. However, you can avoid French probate altogether if you hold your French real estate asset not in your name but in the name of an SCI, which is a French company formed specifically for the purpose of holding property.

You see, therefore, the importance of thinking through ownership structures before making any investment in foreign real estate. Specifically, what are your options?

The first would be to hold the piece of property in your own name. This is the most simple and straightforward strategy and can make sense if you plan to hold the property for only a short period of time. However, generally speaking, this is probably not the best way to hold property in any country. First, it's typically not the best option in the context of the local inheritance laws (as explained in the France example). In addition, though, you want to remember probate. If you hold a piece of property in another country in your name, your heirs will have to go through probate in that country. If you hold property in your name in three other countries, your heirs will have to go through probate in all three. Having to go through probate in a foreign country to claim assets you've left them could change the way your heirs remember you. (You'll be dead, of course, so maybe you don't care.)

That said, there are cases when holding property in your personal name has benefits that override the probate concern. For example, in Argentina and Croatia, if you hold real estate in your personal name (rather than in the name of a corporation), then you are not liable for capital-gains tax when you resell.

The next option for holding real estate is an entity formed within the country where the property is located. As we've mentioned, most buyers in Panama (including Panamanians) take title to their real estate in the name of a Panamanian corporation. This saves you the 2% real estate transfer tax when you resell the property (as long as you hold each property in a separate corporation) and can help to minimize capital-gains taxes. Capital gains in Panama are currently taxed at 10%. However, when you sell your shares of the corporation that owns the real estate, you incur only a 5% withholding on the gross transaction value. Assuming your property has more than doubled in value since you bought it, you can simply opt not to file a tax return on the resale transaction, thereby effectively paying less than 10% on the gain. If the property value hasn't more than doubled, then you file a tax return to request a refund for the difference between the withholding and the actual tax due.

Note that shares of a corporation in a country, while not real estate, are still assets in that country, meaning there still can be a probate risk. The way to avoid that would be to create a parent company or trust to own the local entity. That parent company or trust could be in your home country; however, it can be better from the point of view of asset protection and privacy to use a third jurisdiction for this.

On the other hand, this can be more structuring than you want or need, and layering structures like this can get complicated. Don't attempt it on your own. Seek legal advice both in the country where the property is located and in your home country, especially if you're an American.

The final option for how to hold a piece of property you buy in a foreign country is through a third-country entity. For example, you could take title to your beach house in Nicaragua using a Belizean limited liability company (LLC). Again, however, this can be a more complicated structure than you want or need. In addition, many countries will require you to register the foreign entity locally for tax purposes. This can be difficult for situations in which the country doesn't recognize the type of entity. We struggled with our purchase in Medellín, Colombia, for example, where we were titling in the name of a Nevis LLC. This proved an uncommon approach in this jurisdiction, but our attorney was able to figure it out.

In addition, setting up these kinds of entities comes at a cost. The set-up for a Panamanian corporation costs about $1,200 (depending on the attorney). A Nevis LLC costs about $1,000. Then there are the annual carrying costs, which amount to $550 to $650 for most foreign entities. These costs have to be weighed against the benefits of asset protection, avoiding probate, and minimizing the need for a will in the countries where you want to purchase.

If you are buying only a single piece of real estate in a single country, then the holding structure can and should be simple, maybe just one local entity. The important thing is to understand the tax and estate implications in the country where you're planning to buy and, as well, in your home country before you make a purchase. Changing directions midstream can be expensive. You don't want, for example, to have to retitle a piece of real estate in a foreign country (from your own name to that of an LLC, say). In most cases, this would mean paying the transfer tax again (even if you're transferring the asset from your individual name to that of an entity you own 100%), and the transfer tax can range from 1% to 12% of the property value at the time of the transfer. You want to get the titling right from the start.

25 Manage the Asset—Understanding Your Tax Obligations as an Overseas Property Investor

Property ownership overseas can trigger particular tax liabilities. I've discussed taxes that can be associated with purchasing real estate in a foreign country. However, once you've made the investment, you can also have ongoing associated tax burdens. I'll address the generic ones first (that is, the ones that apply to everyone). Then I'll walk you through the specific U.S. tax implications you'll face as an American buying property overseas.

The most obvious ongoing tax associated with owning a piece of property anywhere is property tax. The good news is that not all countries impose one. If your frame of reference is a U.S. state where the property taxes are high, this can be another nice benefit of diversifying overseas in this way.

Property taxes in many countries are managed at the local level—by the municipality, as it were, which oversees collections and sometimes sets the rates. This means that, depending on the country, you may need to know where, exactly, you'll be buying before you can know what your property tax rates might be. Generally speaking, though, property taxes are lower most everywhere in the world than the U.S. average, and, again, not all countries charge them.

Sometimes, a country exempts certain kinds of properties or certain kinds of purchases from property tax for certain periods of time, to incentivize investment. This has been the case in Panama over the past two decades, when the government offered a 20-year tax exemption to all new property purchases, though this exemption is no longer available on new properties. A property tax exemption or no property tax at all is great, of course, but property tax shouldn't be a determining factor for where you decide to invest and certainly not for where you choose to retire. In most of the world, it's a negligible expense.

Another important consideration when investing in a rental property in another country is that many jurisdictions treat rental income like ordinary income for tax purposes. Typically, you'll have to file a tax return in the country at the end of each year to report your rental income and to show the tax owed. Some countries, though, have figured out that foreign property owners don't always report rental revenues. This has led some countries to impose taxes at the source. Practically speaking, this means that, in some places, your property/rental manager will be meant to hold out some percentage of the rental income you earn and hand it over to the government's tax authority. These withholding rates are typically onerous, with the intent of motivating you to file a full and proper income tax return at the end of the year (hopefully to claim back some of the withholding as a refund).

Our rental property in Portugal fell under this kind of system. The withholding was 25% of the rental revenue after deducting the management fee. The rental manager made the withholding payments for us. These payments turned out to be more than we actually owed each year we owned the property. However, the cost of paying a local accountant to file a tax return to claim back the difference was more than the difference. We were, though, able to claim a credit for the taxes paid in Portugal on our U.S. returns.

Some governments have gone so far as to make the proactive presumption that any nonprimary residence is a rental. They then charge you tax on a presumed rental value/income for your property. Spain does this. With so many foreign property owners who use their condos and villas only part-time and rent them out otherwise, the government wants to be sure it's getting a piece of all the rental income being generated within its jurisdiction. The flaw in this approach is obvious. Not every nonprimary residence is a rental and certainly not every nonprimary residence is rented out full time. If you have a holiday home on the Spanish *costa* that you allow to sit empty when you aren't using it, you won't like this Spanish government tax policy.

Most countries allow you to deduct direct and related expenses against your rental income, including mortgage interest, management expenses, utilities if you're paying them (this would be the case for short-term rentals, for example), and any other direct expenses. What most countries don't allow you to deduct is depreciation. This is a U.S. accounting phenomenon that is also allowed for U.S. tax calculations but typically not elsewhere.

If you are a U.S. citizen holding a rental property in another country, it's treated more or less the same as a U.S. rental property for U.S. tax purposes. You are allowed the same expense deductions, including depreciation (although you have to use a 40-year schedule for non-U.S. property) and the cost of travel to visit and check on the property. You report the rental income on a Schedule E, as you would for any U.S. rental income.

The complications for an American can arise from the tax liability in the country where the property is located. Without depreciation as an expense, you could have a profit in the foreign country and a loss on your U.S. taxes. The tax you pay in the foreign country can be used as a tax credit against any tax owed to Uncle Sam for the same income. If you don't have any net income in the United States, due to depreciation expense, then you have to carry forward the tax credit. Eventually, you may be able to use it. Note, though, that, if you're an American holding foreign property in your own name, that's really the only difference for your U.S. tax-reporting requirements.

VI

How to Sell for Top Dollar

When Lief sold his three-flat building in Chicago, the market was overheated. He listed the property at an inflated price relative to going market rates, thinking he was allowing himself room for negotiation. He got three offers the first weekend, one a bit below the asking price, one a lot below the asking price, and one right on the money.

It was more a seller's market even than Lief had realized. The bidder who came in at full list price had been outbid recently on several other buildings. He wasn't going to lose this one. The amount he agreed to was more than 10% greater than the price the real estate agent had counseled Lief to list at. Fortunately, Lief isn't good at taking advice.

That Chicago experience was a home run for Lief, but you can't count on a frothy market when it comes time to resell a piece of real estate you've invested in overseas. In fact, rarely will the market climate be so strongly in your favor. How, then, can you give yourself the best chance of selling quickly and for maximum return?

Here are our top eight tips.

Resale Tip #1: Don't Buy Common

As the adage goes, in real estate, the money is made in the buy, not the sell. This is true everywhere in the world, and the best way to get top dollar at resale is to avoid common. Choose property with inherent value and premium qualities. This can be about the location, the neighborhood, the building, the development, or the individual asset.

Location is immutable, so be confident in that choice. Other factors are more controllable.

Resale Tip #2: Remember the Importance of Curb Appeal

Years ago, we looked at a house for sale in Panama City. It was in a prime neighborhood, one of the city's best addresses, and the list price reflected that. The owners were so sure they'd be able to sell for top dollar that they made zero effort in advance of listing the property. It was nearly impossible even to walk through the house. The windows were covered by dark, heavy drapes, and every room was cluttered with junk. You couldn't judge the size of the rooms or get any perspective on the place overall. We moved on quickly and noted that the house remained on the market after the family had moved out and into a new house in a new Panama City suburb. That happens a lot with high-end properties in Latin America. Wealthy families don't need to sell so they hold on for top dollar, believing their properties are worth more than they really are, often simply because of where they're located.

The rooms of your rental property overseas probably won't be dark and cluttered, but you should do what you can to make the place inviting. It's tough to change a would-be buyer's first impression, so make it as good as it can be. We've even paid to paint common areas so the approach to our unit was as appealing as possible. Definitely paint your own interior walls if they need it. Make sure the appliances work, especially, in a market in the tropics, the air conditioners (most apartments in Latin America have split-unit air conditioners rather than central air). Even think about upgrading your front door. A heavy, high-quality door can go a long way toward a great first impression, while a screen or hollow, lightweight doors screams cheap.

A potential buyer will favor a property he can list for rental the day he closes without having to do any work. If he perceives the place as rundown, he'll expect a bargain price. Make your property picture perfect, and you can ask top dollar.

Top Tip from Lief

Curb Appeal Is Important When Renting, Too

Doing everything you can to help your property look its best helps when selling, but it helps when trying to find a renter, too. If you're renting long term, repaint between tenants. And check regularly to confirm that all appliances are working. Local landlords often wait until a renter signs a lease before fixing anything. This can put off a savvy renter who understands he can't count on the landlord ever making repairs.

Resale Tip #3: Be Patient

Unless you're selling into a frenzied market, as Lief did in Chicago years ago, patience is another requirement for getting top dollar, especially with a high-end property. Getting your price for a premium property means waiting for the right buyer to come along.

We spend part of each year in Paris, where one of our favorite pastimes is reading the listings in real estate agency windows. Often, the properties highlighted this way are priced higher on a per-square-meter basis than other similar properties in the same neighborhood. This is usually because properties that make it into the agency windows are special in some way. The bargain and more common properties are sold quickly. Those in the windows take longer to sell. If you can be patient to wait for the right buyer to come along, the payoff is worth it.

Resale Tip #4: Invest in Professional Photography

People will come to see the property (or not) based on how it looks on the Internet.

Resale Tip #5: Pick Your Season

Every market has a season that's better for listing and selling than the rest of the year. In some markets, listing in summer versus winter, the dry season rather the wet can make a dramatic difference in the sales price you're able to realize.

Resale Tip #6: Write Your Own Listing

If you have any writing experience or skills, consider drafting copy for the real estate listing yourself. No agent knows your property's selling points as well as you do.

Resale Tip #7: Pay Attention to Your Competition

When selling one of our apartments in Buenos Aires, we noticed that other apartments in the same neighborhood were overpriced, and they weren't selling. We raised our price by $35,000 and were still the cheapest listing in our zone at the time. Our place sold in a matter of days.

Resale Tip #8: Target the Expat Market

The best way to realize a premium when reselling is to sell to another foreigner.

In many markets overseas, including Playa del Carmen in Mexico and most towns along the cost of Spain, for example, the buying pool is primarily expats. In a market like Medellín, Colombia, however, with more local than foreign demand, you should do everything you can to connect with potential foreign buyers. You'll almost always be able to charge more than if selling on the local market.

Decorate your property to be attractive to a North American and promote the property online in English and through an English-speaking real estate agent. Listing with an English-speaking agent who markets exclusively to North Americans is like advertising your property in the window of a Paris agency. It will attract buyers looking for a simple, turnkey purchase and willing to pay more not to have to do any work. The best buyer is one who doesn't have or who isn't willing to take the time to hunt for a bargain. That's almost always a foreign buyer.

VII

How Not to Lose Money—Confessions of a Couple of Overseas Property Investors Who Have Made Costly Mistakes

One big loss can wipe out a lot of gains. After more than two-and-a-half decades of property investing experience across 24 countries, we have learned that the hard way six times over. Here are the stories of our biggest failures, the investments that stand out in memory as having cost us and taught us most. We share them so you can learn these lessons before putting any of your own money at risk.

26 Don't Be Tempted to Take a Second Bite

The greatest real estate loss of our investing careers earned that position of honor thanks to good, old-fashioned greed. This one was all Lief. Kathleen was never on board. Just like every other investor we knew, Lief got caught up in the exuberance of global markets in the years leading up to the 2008 global real estate crisis and double dipped, despite Kathleen's reluctance.

A colleague had a brother. His brother had a friend who was working with a developer in Northern England. The project fit all the parameters of a great deal. It was preconstruction, so the pricing was below market. The payment terms were the standard of the day—10% down with two more 10% payments over XX months. The developer had lined up banks to finance the remaining 70% upon completion. The rental-income projections were conservative based on current rents and would slightly better than cover the mortgage and other operating expenses. On paper, the deal was golden. Lief reserved one of the condos.

A colleague invested, too, and, after we'd made our initial deposits, he updated us regularly on sales and general progress with the project. A few months after we'd made the purchase, the colleague sent an email saying that 10 units had come back onto the market. A group of Italian investors had fallen out.

By that time, the developer had increased prices, which is typical with this kind of preconstruction offer. To create momentum and to get cash flowing, preconstruction developers offer sometimes significantly discounted prices at the initial launch phase. As sales are made, they increase prices according to a predetermined schedule. After X units have sold, prices are increased by Y%, and so on. As the units that came back onto the market for the development of our colleague's brother's friend had been sold at launch, the developer was offering them to other buyers in the project not at that original price but at a nicely reduced cost compared with the current going rate.

Lief broke out his calculator and spreadsheet to remind himself of the numbers behind the deal and got himself so excited that he decided to take a second bite at the profits he projected. Buying a second apartment in the same building violated our personal diversification rules, but the numbers were that good. Plus, we had the cash in hand for another down payment and no other compelling opportunity on our radar competing for it.

When we tell this story to other investors, they interject at this point to say, "Aha … but then the developer didn't complete. The building didn't get built." That's the most common reason preconstruction deals go south. But that's not what happened here. The building was delivered on time, but the timing was colossally bad. It was 2007. Newcastle, England, where the project was located, like many markets at the time, was overbuilt. This global oversupply had a lot to do with the historic bust of property markets worldwide a year later.

We had never been to Newcastle. When our units were completed, we decided to make the trip to see the apartments firsthand and to work with the management company to furnish and list them for rental. We'd been told that the building's location was prime, and the building style and amenities were intended to target the local hip and upwardly mobile crowd. Those things could have been true, but we realized they weren't the point within three minutes of getting out of our rental car and walking down the high street. Newcastle was grey and depressed, shabby and rundown. We saw no reason to stick around and no reason to return. How many upwardly mobile types could there be shopping in this town for hip digs?

When we met with him, the rental management agent wasn't optimistic about getting the rents that had been projected two years earlier. Indeed, he cautioned us that we might struggle to find renters at all in the current climate. Several other buildings nearby and in other locations around the city had recently been completed. It was not a landlord's market.

We had financed the 70% balance due on our two apartments. We were committed and instructed the management agent to do his best to get the units rented so the cash flow could begin covering the mortgages. To our relief, both apartments rented quickly but for 75% of the monthly rents we'd been expecting. We figured we'd be fine. We'd increase the rents the next year, as Lief had done every year with his Chicago apartments. If only.

One tenant moved out at the end of the first year, and we weren't able to replace him. The other renter stayed on, but the market forced us to lower the rents for both apartments. Not significantly but enough to turn our cash flow negative. We were paying out of pocket to cover expenses. At the end of the second year, the rental manager told us we needed to reduce the rents further. Rental rates continued down as more inventory continued coming onto the market.

Not only had rents fallen due to oversupply over the two years since we'd taken possession of our apartments, but so, too, had property values. Local agents counseled us that the best sales prices we could hope for were about 75% of what we'd paid for each unit. Backing out real estate commissions and other costs, we wouldn't be left with enough to cover the amounts owed on the mortgages.

Lief called the bank that was carrying the loans to try to renegotiate terms. While our loans were amortizing, interest-only mortgages were common in the UK at the time. We figured the bank would rather switch us to an interest-only payment rather than take the properties back. We were wrong.

It was still early in the real estate crash, and the bank refused to talk to us about options. We can only guess that they became more flexible as their books filled with the properties of fellow investors who likewise couldn't sustain their debts over the following 12 months.

That left us in a painful position. We had a choice to make. We could sell at a loss and then come up with more money out of pocket to pay back the mortgages. We could continue to cover the negative cash flow, which was expanding each year rather than shrinking. Or we could walk away and let the lender have it all. We made good-faith efforts to work with the bank, and they told us to take a hike.

The total loss was the 30% down payment on each apartment plus the closing costs, the furnishing costs, and the cash we'd injected to cover expenses for about 14 months. We've not experienced another loss of this caliber before nor since.

Rather than double dipping and buying the second apartment, we should have put 60% down on one apartment. With that level of financing, the cash flow would have been positive even with the falling rents. The investment would have underperformed expectations, but it would not have been a complete loss. Over time, as the local property market recovered, we could have come out okay.

This was our first lesson in the dangers of leverage. Previous experiences in Chicago and Spain and many leveraged investments since have been casebook successes. It was this one, where we doubled down, that blew up.

However, the biggest lesson we learned from this Newcastle debacle was never to invest in a market you do not know and have not scouted personally. Even if it's preconstruction purchase and a boots-on-the-ground inspection trip amounts to standing in a vacant lot, make the trip. Walk the neighborhood. Look to see what else is being built in the vicinity. Speak with the locals about the path of development and the state of the economy. See for yourself the commerce taking place (or not) in the shops and restaurants.

Had we made the quick trip from Waterford, Ireland, where we were living at the time, to Northern England, to spend a day in Newcastle, we would not have made this investment. We would have ignored Lief's spreadsheet and projections. Cash-flow math is key to making good cash-flow investment decisions, but so too is your personal understanding of market dynamics.

Lesson Learned

Don't buy in a market you don't know personally without getting on a plane to see it for yourself first.

27

Know Who You're Buying With

In the early 2000s, we met a young entrepreneur in Nicaragua whose family owned a piece of land on a lake. He'd begun, with family money, to develop the land into a resort. He had no prior development or construction experience. The lack of construction experience didn't bother us. You can hire that out. And we didn't worry about the lack of development experience because his vision was strong and his family backed him, because it had the financial resources and the local connections to follow through. The location was excellent, and the guy had prioritized the lakeside amenities—a restaurant, bar, and activity area—which were already in place when we visited for the first time. This was smart; these kinds of services help foster rentals.

The developer positioned the product as turnkey. The bungalow investment would be supported by rental and property management. As an owner, you bought your unit then waited for your income checks. That was the promise.

We invested early then watched, over a couple of years, as the developer sold a couple dozen more bungalows. Construction was slow at times, both because construction is always slow at times in the developing world and also because in this case roads and foundations were being dug from the side of a caldera. The dramatic setting was a big part of why we bought. Still, the developer stayed reasonably on schedule.

After our bungalow was completed, we visited to create a punch list of construction items to finalize and to furnish the place. We discovered that the developer wasn't offering furnishing packages. He didn't recognize the value of keeping all the bungalows similar or recognize that putting the burden of furnishing on the owners interfered with his representation of this as a turnkey proposition. That was our first clue that rental and property management hadn't been thought through.

We bought tables, chairs, beds, mattresses, televisions, bedsheets, towels, and so forth, as did the other buyers whose units were completed. Construction continued farther up the hill on additional bungalows, but, with the first 10 built and ready for guests, the developer announced the grand opening of the resort.

And nothing happened. No bookings. None at all. The restaurant and bar continued to attract tourists to the lake, but they came for lunch or dinner. No one was staying overnight.

What was the problem?

The developer had no marketing plan. His strategy was build it and guests will come. He didn't begin to think about how to fill the bungalows until after they'd been completed.

This was before VRBO (Vacation Rentals by Owner) and Airbnb. Travel agencies were still a key part of the travel industry, and that's where this developer went to try to drum up business. He planned travel trade excursions and fam trips, inviting agents to stay at the property with the hope they'd recommend it to their clients. He met with Nicaragua's Ministry of Tourism to try to get them to include the resort in their materials. He made reasonable efforts, but it was too little too late. Months, then a year passed with just a handful of bookings, and the developer had sold and was building 30 more bungalows.

The developer's biggest problem, we can see now, was a reluctance to delegate. He was involved in all decisions, no matter how small. Running a construction project and running a hotel are both full-time jobs. He was trying to fill both roles at the same time, and he had experience in neither.

Over the next couple of years, as the remaining bungalows were completed, occupancy picked up slightly, but the developer burned out. He was managing complaints from early owners upset about the low rental yields while fielding questions and concerns from new buyers. It was too much for any one man to handle. Finally, he succumbed to pressure to engage an experienced rental manager. The decision, again, was made too late, and the pool of labor he had to draw from was limited. He engaged an expat couple whose experience amounted to managing a couple of houses in nearby Granada as short-term rentals.

Then came the final nail in the coffin. We learned that the developer hadn't formalized the homeowner's association (HOA). HOA fees had been increased to cover the salary of the new rental managers, but, when owners realized they weren't legally obliged to make their monthly HOA payments, they stopped. No one wanted to cover the rental management costs when there was next to no rental income. Unable to draw their salary from the HOA funds, the management team moved on, leaving the place in a bigger mess than it had been in before they took over.

By this time, the developer had bailed, too. To his credit and though he was under no obligation to do so, he signed over the amenities to the homeowners before walking away. The restaurant and bar threw off a small stream of income but not enough to compensate for the rental cash flow that never materialized.

We eventually sold our bungalow for $1 to someone who lived in Nicaragua and was up for managing the property as a rental personally. He planned to extricate it from the completely non-functional group management program. Fortunately, the investment wasn't large so the loss wasn't painful, just humbling.

Analyzing the experience now, nearly 20 years later, we agree that the premise was sound. The developer owned the land and had no debt. The family had the wherewithal to build out the infrastructure and the amenities. What we paid for was delivered; our bungalow was built.

However, the developer flat out had no business acting as a resort manager and was too slow to give up control and engage professional help.

What are the important takeaways? One is not to let a failed investment like this one turn you off making another similar investment in the future. This Nicaraguan developer was trying to build what would be considered a condo-hotel. Condo hotels can and do work. The most successful ones sign a hotel brand for the marketing and have an experienced management company in place before breaking ground.

Had this opportunity been presented as buy a bungalow and rent it out rather than as a turnkey rental investment, it could have been successful. The developer could have focused on building and managing the resort amenities, and owners could have handled their rental units as they saw fit.

If the project were built today, the developer would have the benefit of online marketing to support his rental program. Airbnb and Booking.com have helped to make small rental projects like this one more viable.

Lesson Learned

Confirm that the developer has relevant experience and is supported by a professional team.

28 Understand the Local Bureaucracy

Things like real estate laws, zoning, types of title, and how you can hold title can vary state to state in the United States but in ways that are seldom meaningful to individual investors. The differences when investing overseas can be significant, compared with both U.S. legislation, regulations, and restrictions, and country to country.

The United States uses common law; most countries where you'll be interested in investing overseas use civil law. This has big implications. You can't assume, for example, when making a purchase with your spouse, that, because both names are on the title, you are taking ownership as joint tenants with rights of survivorship. That doesn't exist everywhere.

A guy we knew in Colombia decided to develop a coffee plantation and sell individual parcels within it to investors. A farm manager would manage the plantation. He promised each investor title to his parcel. The investors would get cash flow from harvest sales plus branded coffee as part of their return. The vision was appealing and fun.

The developer had done his due diligence on global coffee markets, farm prices in Colombia, and the equipment, labor, and infrastructure needed for processing harvests, and he even started an import/export company so he could ship his coffee production to North America.

He bought two coffee farms totaling about 40 hectares. One had a processing facility on it. Both had land beyond what had been planted, allowing for expansion.

He marketed quarter-acre parcels (1,000 square meters, or one-tenth of a hectare). The sales price was affordable, and he sold a lot of parcels quickly. The project took off. He toured investors at the farms, showing off his facilities for processing the coffee beans, even staging coffee-tasting classes and awarding certificates for the best noses and palates.

Meanwhile, he engaged surveyors to create the segregation plan for the quarter-acre parcels. When that work was finished, he presented the plan to the local land office for approval. That's when he discovered he had a problem. The minimum allowable size for a piece of rural property in that municipality of Colombia was five hectares. He wasn't going to be able to title the quarter-acre parcels he'd promised and sold to his investors.

Not that he accepted that reality easily or quickly. He spent a lot of time and money on attorneys and speaking with local officials. Finally, though, he had to concede that he wasn't going to be able to give individual titles to his buyers. He and his lawyers came up with a creative alternative plan. They presented each investor with a title to whichever of the two coffee properties he'd bought into with every individual investor's percentage of ownership listed out. Not the same as an individual title but a reasonable resolution.

One might take from that story that five hectares is the standard allowable minimum size for rural property in Colombia. It isn't.

Every five years, each municipality in Colombia (and in other Latin American countries, too) publishes what's referred to as an Esquema de Ordenamiento Territorial (EOT). The EOT is the development plan for the municipality and lays out zoning rules, minimum allowable parcel sizes, and land use requirements. These things vary municipality by municipality and are reconsidered every five years.

Another colleague developed a series of timber plantations in another region of Colombia. As part of his planning, he checked into the local EOT. In this much more rural region of Colombia, with hundreds of thousands of hectares of virgin land, the minimum parcel size for an individual title is 300 hectares. Most parcels in the region are 1,000 hectares or more.

Brazil, Uruguay, and Argentina, likewise, impose restrictions ranging from the minimum allowable sizes for rural properties to how much productive or rural land can be owned by foreigners. In Brazil, foreigners can't own more than a certain percentage of the total area of each state. This means it's critical to check locally before buying agricultural land, for example, to confirm that the piece you're purchasing doesn't push the total amount of foreign-owned land in that state over the allowable limit.

Argentina has restrictions on the total amount of land that can be owned by foreigners and also requires foreigners buying in an area considered a security zone to apply for permission first. For the Argentines, the security zones are the country's international borders, primarily the border with Chile.

Our apartment in Medellín, when we bought it, was across the street from a cute little Spanish-style house that had been converted to a small shop selling snacks and sandwiches. This was possible because of a lack of zoning restriction against opening a business in an otherwise 100% residential neighborhood. Zoning is not a thing in Latin America.

On a visit a year after we'd bought and renovated the property, we saw that the little house across the street had been torn down. We had come to rely on the shop for snacks and had gotten to know the owner and his family. Why was the house torn down, we asked our neighbors. The response helped to explain why Medellín is such a green city. Medellín, in its EOT, requires a minimum number of square meters of park area per capita.

When a developer erects a high-rise apartment building in this city, if the number of potential residents of the building upsets the balance between park area and people, the developer is obliged to build a park. When a developer faced this situation in our neighborhood, he bought the little house across the street from our place, tore it down, and made a park. Initially, it was more an open field than a bona-fide park area. As developers have built more apartments in our zone, each has been required to invest in expanding and improving the park. In the years we've owned our apartment, the next two houses adjacent to the former sandwich shop have been purchased by developers and torn down, as well. Trees and shrubs have been planted. Benches have been installed. We miss our little sandwich shop but now appreciate the nice green space.

The park rule in Medellín was a pleasant surprise. Other consequences of a lack of zoning we've encountered over the years have been less so. We knew a couple who bought a house in a quiet neighborhood of Cuenca, Ecuador, only to have a discotheque open up next door. The music blasted until the wee hours. Calls to the police did no good. The nightclub wasn't breaking any laws.

In markets where zoning laws exist, they can change after you've bought. A friend owned a small villa near the coast in the Algarve region of Portugal for decades. She and her family used it for family holidays and personal vacations. Eventually, they found they weren't getting to the house as often as they once had. The now grown kids didn't want their parents to sell, so the couple decided to set the place up for short-term rental to generate cash flow when not being used by the family.

They'd bought in the 1970s, when zoning rules in this part of Portugal weren't restrictive and the government was too busy navigating the depression the country was suffering through to worry about the pace of development on its Algarve coast. However, by the 2000s, the government began paying attention, and, in an effort to prevent its beautiful Adriatic coast from devolving into something like Spain's Costa del Sol, changed the zoning rules. When our friend and her husband decided to add a pool in the back yard to make the house more rentable, they found that the new regulations mandated no new construction within 500 meters of the coast. The area for their would-be pool fell within that zone. They were denied a permit. Without a pool, the property was not competitive as a rental, and selling it wouldn't be easy.

You aren't going to be able to imagine every change or improvement you might like to make to a property over the lifetime of your ownership. Nor can you predict how a country or a region is going to change its zoning laws. So, before buying, ask yourself if the property serves the intended purposes and will be able to meet the expected cash flow projections as is, understanding that as is may be all there ever is. A tourist rental at the beach typically needs a swimming pool. If the property you're considering buying doesn't have a pool and you don't plan to invest in adding a pool immediately (assuming you've confirmed you'd be able to do that), then maybe shop for another property that'd make for a more competitive rental.

Lesson Learned

Don't assume that the laws to do with ownership, taking title, and zoning in the place where you're buying overseas are the same as you know them to be back home. They will almost always be different.

29 Be Sure of Your Exit Market

When investing in a residential rental property in the United States, you have a good idea who your future buyer will be. You'll sell, when the time comes, to someone looking to live in that neighborhood or to another investor shopping for a rental property in that area. Either way, the buyer likely will be someone living within a couple dozen miles.

When buying for cash flow in another country, especially a short-term rental unit, the location and the type of property play big roles in determining who your potential future buyer will be. Typically, your potential future buyer pool will include other foreign investors. However, the more you can expand that pool, the greater your chances for maximum return.

The Spanish *costas* are a good example of a market that has relied on foreign buyers and investors entirely. In 2008, when real estate markets across the globe collapsed, those along Spain's Mediterranean coast fell faster and harder than any others. There were three reasons for this—the amount of leverage in play, overbuilding, and the fact that the majority of buyers on this coast were foreign.

Prices fell, too, at the time, in Barcelona, but not nearly as far nor for as long as they did along the *costas*. The three factors that spelled disaster on the coast helped to insulate values in Barcelona. The percentage of leveraged investment properties was lower, the volume of overconstruction was less, and the market didn't rely on foreign money.

Even along the *costas*, owners of well-positioned properties of interest saw their values recover quicker than owners of cookie-cutter units in the massive oceanside complexes where dozens and hundreds of identical properties came onto the market from distressed sellers overnight.

We remembered stories we'd heard about the collapse of Spain's coastal markets when shopping for an investment in Portugal in 2015. Local real estate agents convinced us to consider apartments in resort complexes. The rental returns on these showed well on spreadsheets. Projections showed that we could have netted 8% on almost every unit we viewed. We reminded ourselves, though, that the rental return was just one criterion to consider. What about when we wanted to use the property ourselves? And what about when the time came to sell?

Kathleen prioritizes character and charm in any purchase. In this case, though, even Lief had to agree that these hundreds of all-the-same resort condos rubbed me the wrong way. And we both worried we'd never be able to find our apartment in one of these complexes of hundreds of lookalike units.

Of greater concern to me was the thought of competing with hundreds of other sellers of exactly the same product should another market downfall mean many owners become sellers at once. Even in a good market, how would we compete for a sale with whatever other units were available at the same time other than on price?

Touring several resort complexes reminded us we're not resort complex types. We focused instead on the center of the coastal town of Lagos, where we found a one-of-a-kind townhouse on a winding pedestrian-only cobblestoned street with a rooftop terrace with a view of the ocean. Standing on that roof we knew we'd look forward to every chance to return to stay in the property ourselves and with our children. And we also knew that, when we decided to sell, we'd have something with intrinsic value to offer that would compete handily with anything else available at the time, boom market or bust.

That nature of the property meant an expanded future resale market. The townhouse was ideal for a short-term rental but comfortable for full-time living, too. It would be attractive to another foreign investor but also to an expat wanting to retire on this coast or to a local living and working in the city. When, four years after the purchase, we decided to cash out of what we perceived to be a market at a top, our buyer was a retired couple from Sweden that planned to use the property part of the year and rent it out otherwise.

In some markets, you'll have no choice but to resell to a foreigner. Ambergris Caye, Belize, is a good example. Most of the construction on this island is geared toward the tourist and expat retiree markets. Beachfront condos aren't in the budget for a typical Belizean local. The economies you need to pay attention to if you invest in a cash flow property on Ambergris are in North America.

When the United States falls into recession, fewer properties are sold on Ambergris Caye. When U.S. markets are booming, more real estate is sold on this little Isla Bonita. The local Belize economy is irrelevant. Same goes for rental returns. Most rentals are to North Americans and some European tourists.

Buy right in a market like Ambergris, and you can see good rental yields until the economy slows in the countries your tourist renters hail from. And, when your occupancy stats fall, so will your ability to sell the asset quickly or at a decent price.

Paris, on the other hand, is a market where you're lucky to earn better than a 5% net rental yield from a rental, but you'll always be able to resell your property. Prices move up and down in Paris. Like anywhere, the market cycles. Still, you'll always find a buyer. The potential future buyer pool in this city is as wide as it gets and includes other investors, foreigners wanting their own *pieds-à-terre* in the City of Light, and local French buyers.

The point is that it's critical to size up your future potential buyer pool in advance of a purchase. However, some opportunities are predicated on an expectation that that pool is going to expand for some specific reason.

In the early 2000s, a developer we knew in Canada subdivided a rural oceanfront parcel into large estate lots and offered them for sale to investor buyers based on a path-of-progress pitch. He postulated that, because country properties in the far northeastern United States, in Vermont and Maine, known for attracting wealthy weekend-home buyers out of Boston, Connecticut, and New York, had become too expensive, those buyers would begin looking at Nova Scotia, Canada, to satisfy their country estate appetites once the ferry route between Bay Harbor, Maine, and Yarmouth, Nova Scotia, reopened, as, he said, it was soon to do.

But the path-of-progress play didn't play out. The ferry did not reopen as expected, the United States went into recession, and Nova Scotia has a lot of raw coastal land. Even as we write, that ferry isn't operating due to renovation work at the Bar Harbor terminal.

The nonfunctioning ferry left investors in this development, including me, with the local market as the only viable potential buyer pool. Nova Scotia has a population density comparable to that of Maine, and Maine has the lowest population density of any state in the United States. In other words, not a big potential buyer pool for estate parcels to build vacation homes.

Lesson Learned

Think through the future potential buyer pool when making any cash-flow investment and choose properties that expand that pool as much as possible.

30 Manage Your Rental Manager

I've owned rental properties in eight countries. The property is important. You need to buy right—right location, right size, right number of bedrooms and bathrooms, right furnishings, and so forth. However, at least as important as the rental you purchase is the person you hire to manage it. A good rental manager can squeeze a good or great return from a so-so property, but, if your manager is no good, you will not make money, no matter how ideal your property.

Finding a good rental manager isn't easy. In some markets, it's not possible. If the rental market is thin, no serious management industry develops. Whoever you find, even if they are experienced and professional, you'll need to invest time launching them and then you'll need to pay attention over time. Leave a rental manager on their own without checking in with them regularly (I recommend at least once a month) can lead to depressed returns.

Our first experiences engaging a rental manager were in Paris. We invested in an apartment with friends and were responsible for getting it rented. The agent who'd sold us the apartment told us she knew the best rental manager in the city. We didn't know any rental managers in this city, so we went with the agent's recommendation. We furnished the place, decorated according to the advice of the manager woman, and then turned the apartment over to her.

A month later, Lief noticed an unexpected transfer into our bank account. The money had come from the rental manager in Paris. It was the net from our first month's income. Exciting surprise to have money show up out of the blue like that, but what did the amount represent? We contacted the manager woman and asked for a report. We explained that we wanted to see rental dates, gross amounts paid, and expenses deducted. The typical data points any rental property owner should want to review and that you need to calculate occupancy rates, to track your yield, and to control your expenses.

We didn't receive a report, but more money appeared in our account about four weeks later.

This continued for months. Finally, we reached out to the agent who'd sold us the apartment. She was a friend of the manager woman. Would she, we asked, please request a report for us. She did, but what we received wasn't much better than no information at all. Meanwhile money continued posting to our account monthly.

After 12 months, we totaled our annual net income and calculated the annual net yield for the property. It was 5.3%, which is good for Paris. Still, we had no idea about the occupancy rate, what the manager woman was charging on a nightly basis, or what costs were being backed out. Was the agent reporting all the income? Was she charging market rates? Was she padding expenses?

After about a year-and-a-half of this uncomfortably murky situation, we were introduced to another rental manager in Paris who was looking to add to his rental portfolio. We interviewed him and explained our concerns about our current manager. He assured us that he'd send monthly reports showing all the details we were looking for, so we switched to the new guy.

He sent reports as promised, in the format we'd requested, but our cash flow plunged. Occupancy rates were easy to calculate some months because they were zero. This new manager was much more organized than the old one had been. He just couldn't rent the apartment.

If you have to choose, which would you rather have? Reliable reporting or cash in the bank? You hope you never have to ask yourself that question. We learned from this early experience that, if a rental manager is producing healthy cash flow, think long and hard before making any changes. If the situation isn't broken in the one way that really matters (the amounts of net cash flow being earned), don't try to fix it.

We ask for (insist on) reports from every rental manager we work with, and you should, too, but, if the agent is keeping the place rented, we're willing to work with them to improve their administrative skills.

The second place we invested in a rental property was Buenos Aires, Argentina, where, in 2002, about six months after the decoupling of the Argentine peso from the U.S. dollar and the resulting collapse of the peso, we purchased three apartments with friends. It was a casebook crisis investing window, and we were able to buy three classic-style Buenos Aires properties at prime addresses for pennies on the peso.

The real estate agency we used told us they were starting an in-house rental management company to service the growing number of international clients investing at the time. As in Paris, we didn't know any rental managers in Buenos Aires, so this agency option seemed a good turnkey solution.

The woman put in charge of the business set up marketing, administration, and reporting infrastructure quickly and was filling the apartments with renters within a month. Reports came regularly, as did deposits into the bank account. The investment was a success at every level. For the first two years. The woman running the management division of the agency's operations was also the wife of the agency owner. After she'd established the rental management business, she reverted to working with her husband in the (bigger and more lucrative) sales division. The couple hired a young woman to take over rental management. This woman was competent enough but didn't have the same personal commitment to making things work.

Reporting became less regular, and communication waned. A year after the transition, after having requested an updated rental report for months, we received one only to find that one of the three apartments hadn't been rented for two months. Not a single night. When we responded to ask why the apartment was suddenly empty for two full months, the woman replied, "Well, I can't rent it with all that water damage in the master bedroom."

This was the first we'd heard about the leak that, by this time, had nearly collapsed the bedroom ceiling. The manager told me she was waiting for the ceiling to be repaired before placing renters in the apartment again. But how, we wondered, was the ceiling going to get repaired if she never told us about the damage? We started looking for a new rental manager.

How do you find a good rental manager? Interview more than one. Lay out your expectations directly. You want to receive monthly reporting showing the number of nights rented, the amount of gross revenue, itemized expenses (including utilities, cleaning, repairs, maintenance, and building fees), the management fee, and the resulting net cash flow to you. You want to receive immediate notification of property damage or a tenant problem or complaint. You want to receive your net cash flow deposited into your bank account monthly or quarterly. Then ask the rental manager candidate for references. Contact at least two other current clients. If the manager candidate won't give you references, find another candidate to consider.

Lesson Learned

Choosing a rental manager is as important as choosing the rental property.

---

31 Remember the Fundamentals

When we arrived in Ireland in 1998, the standard net return from a rental property was 2% or less. The country was a decade into its Celtic Tiger economic boom, which had been fueled by two things. The first was American businesses setting up shop in Ireland to take advantage of low corporate tax rates and hiring incentives being offered by the government. The second was real estate.

Indeed, we were in Ireland for the first reason. We'd made the move to open an office for a U.S. publishing company wanting in on the Irish Investment and Development Agency's 10% tax.

All the foreign business activity created an employment boom. For the first time in the country's history, young Irish were able to leave their parents' houses before they got married. They could afford to live on their own or with roommates. This phenomenon created an unprecedented housing demand. Developers bought land from farmers to build housing estates, and the farmers gave some of those windfall land profits to their kids so they could buy houses. A lending industry emerged. Mortgage broker offices popped up on the street corners of every town and village across the country.

All of Ireland were buying and selling property either for their own uses or, eventually, as investments. The whole of the country watched prices rise dramatically year after year after year and felt compelled to get in on the game. No one imagined an end to the cycle.

It was a house of cards that eventually collapsed completely. One Irish friend who jumped in at the late stages of the boom and bought a house in 2006 to live in with his family has been upside down in the mortgage for that house for more than a decade. At least he's been able to keep up with the mortgage payments. Many pre-2008 Irish buyers have not been so fortunate.

Hardest hit were those who'd bought for investment. So many of these properties were taken back by banks, which had lent as much as 110% of the purchase price, the extra 10% to cover closing costs.

Every Irish investor at the time bought with the expectation that they'd make their return from appreciation. They ignored the fundamentals of property investing and abandoned common sense, buying into the going belief that property prices would continue up indefinitely.

It wasn't only the Irish infected by this disease pre-2008. We met an American property investor back then who bragged to me that he controlled $2 million worth of property. He had made initial payments of $5,000 on eight $250,000 condos. His plan was to resell one or two condos at a time to come up with the next payment due on the rest. He'd created a leveraged ladder that he believed would turn his $40,000 into a small fortune.

Then came the crash of 2008. The guy couldn't sell his condos for a reasonable price or at all. He lost all eight properties, along with his $40,000. Like all those Irish investors, he'd counted on perpetually appreciating market values. That's La La Land.

The key fundamental that too many property investors ignore or maybe aren't aware of, both pre-2008 and, alas, today, is that a rental property should generate enough rental income to give you positive cash flow and a decent net yield. Those are the two critical requirements for any successful rental investment. Do not buy a rental property for any reason other than because you are confident both of those things are going to play out.

We look for a net yield from a rental investment of 5% to 8%. We do not make a purchase unless we believe, based on reliable market data, that we can realistically expect a net return of at least 5%. If a property produces less than a net of 5% a year, we reevaluate to understand what has shifted in the market and, depending on the value of the asset, can consider cashing out so we can put that capital to work elsewhere. If a property produces more than 8% net a year, we count ourselves lucky but understand that the situation won't last. You net more than 8% from a rental only as a result of some market distortion that sooner rather than later will return to the mean.

If you're earning net cash flow of 5% to 8% a year from a rental, that investment is solid. Maybe you're realizing capital appreciation, as well, but trying to predict value growth is speculation. Buying for positive cash flow is building wealth.

Lesson Learned

The projected net return from cash flow should be the primary determining factor when making any property investment overseas.

What Every Overseas Property Buyer Needs to Know About Transferring Money Across Borders in Our Post-FATCA, Anti-money-laundering Age

K ey to buying a piece of real estate in another country is getting the cash required to close the sale where it needs to be when it needs to be there. In fact, as a would-be overseas property owner, you potentially face three international money management requirements. First when you buy; second if you renovate; and third when managing a property as a rental.

The most important thing to understand before wiring money to another country is whether that country imposes currency restrictions. Most don't, but, if the country where you intend to buy real estate does, you want to understand the restrictions before committing to a purchase. This is something to discuss and clarify with your local attorney. Colombia, for example, requires that any incoming funds be registered with the country's central bank. If the funds are for living expenses, for example, then you complete one form (Form 4). If the funds are for investment, then you complete a different form (Form 5), indicating what type of investment you're making. Complete the incorrect form or fail to file one at all, and you will have a difficult time repatriating your capital and any associated profits. Complete and file all the paperwork correctly, and you should have no problem taking your money back out of the country if and when you decide you'd like to.

Brazil imposes similar rules. In this case, though, friends who've bought in this country report that, even if all the paperwork has been processed as called for, it still can be difficult to get your money out. Argentina had such strict controls in place at one point that getting any hard currency out of that country was all but impossible. Selling your property to someone with funds outside the country became the easiest way around the restrictions. While this works in your favor when selling, be careful when buying this way in a country with currency controls. You don't want to end up with a higher tax burden when you sell because you can't prove the provenance of the original investment capital.

Escrow doesn't exist in most of the world. This is because title companies don't exist in most of the world, and title companies handle escrow. Typically, therefore, when purchasing real estate in another country, you'll send the required funds to your *notaire* or your attorney who, depending on the country, might have a client escrow account. This can work if you trust your attorney with that much money (even an honest guy can be tempted to retire early if enough money is made available to him). Another, sometimes safer option can be to send the funds to your own bank account in the country and have your bank issue a certified check to hand over to the seller at closing. If you can get the seller to agree, you can try to use a U.S. escrow company, but most sellers in most of the world won't understand what "escrow" is, and, if they do, they won't like the idea of the funds for the closing sitting in another country. In the case of Argentina, the currency house you're using for the transaction effectively acts as the escrow company.

No matter the final solution, you'll be wiring the funds required. Some online banking systems allow you to initiate a wire from your account online, but, if you're new to international wires, we recommend going into your bank branch to request the wire and fill out the paperwork in person. The timing is important, as you'll need to initiate the wire in time to allow the funds to arrive well in advance of the closing date. Depending on the routing, a wire from a U.S. bank to a Latin American bank can arrive the same day, or it can take up to a week. Wires to Europe typically take three to five business days. Much can depend on the correspondent bank. With one, the wire might arrive the same day; with another, it could take up to five days. Much, too, depends on the receiving bank. Some banks post incoming wires to the client's account within 24 hours; others hold the money in limbo for a few days. There's nothing you can do about this except be informed and prepared.

To send a wire, you'll need instructions from the receiving bank, whether it's your own bank or that of your attorney or *notaire*. Financial institutions in the United States use mostly American Bankers' Association (ABA) numbers for in-country transfers and SWIFT numbers for incoming international wires. The international bank account number (IBAN) system, used mostly in Europe, is more efficient, as the coding for an IBAN number references both your bank and your account information, minimizing the risk of misrouting.

The wire instructions may include information about the recipient bank's correspondent bank or intermediary bank. Much of the time this isn't necessary, though, because banks can access this information on their own. Most banks work with more than one intermediary bank, so don't be alarmed if the wire instructions you're provided include options or a chain of banks.

Increasingly, any sending bank is going to ask for full address details for the recipient bank and the owner of the recipient bank account. The sending bank may require phone numbers for both, as well. It's best to ask your bank what details it requires for an international wire before making a transfer request to avoid it being denied.

If you're wiring the funds to your attorney's client account, notify your attorney when you request the wire. Provide him with details of the sending bank and the amount of the wire, so that he's able to confirm receipt with his bank and make sure the funds are properly credited to you.

Note that if you purchase preconstruction, you'll have a series of money management requirements. You'll make a down payment when you sign the purchase agreement, then you'll make staged payments to the developer throughout the construction process, with one final payment due at closing. In the case of a preconstruction purchase from a developer, you can opt to wire funds directly to the developer. This works as long as the country imposes no currency or flow of funds restrictions (most countries where you'd be interested in buying don't), and it simplifies things, removing one layer of risk. In the case of Colombia or Brazil, however, or any other country that does impose currency controls, the best option is typically to wire funds into your or your attorney's account so that you can be certain the money is properly registered. Then arrange a transfer from your or your attorney's account to that of the developer.

If you purchase a place that requires renovation work, you'll have additional money-management requirements. You'll need to get money into the country as required to cover the associated costs. In this case, you'll need your own local bank account to which to wire funds and from which to pay your contractor, electrician, plumber, carpenter, and so forth.

Sometimes It Makes Sense to "Buy Ahead"

If you're intending to send a big amount of funds of one currency (say U.S. dollars) to a country where the currency is something else, you have an exchange issue that could work in your favor, or not. You shouldn't try to time currency movements. You can't. Nobody can. You can, though, if you deem it prudent, eliminate future currency risk by locking in a current rate of exchange. You can also make sure you get the best possible rate of exchange at the time you transfer your funds. You accomplish both these things by running the money you intend to transfer through a foreign exchange house.

Say you want to buy an apartment in Paris or a farmhouse in Tuscany. You'll need euros. Wire the money for the purchase from your U.S. bank account directly to Europe (either to an account you hold there or to your attorney or *notaire's* account), and, in most cases, your U.S. bank will exchange your U.S. dollars into euros before making the transfer. The more money you send, the better exchange rate the bank will give you, but, generally speaking, the rate of exchange used won't be the best possible or even good. For small wires, it may not be worth the trouble, but, if you're sending a sizable amount, you could benefit significantly from the better rate of exchange available from a foreign exchange company. The difference between the conversion rate used by your bank and the one used by a foreign exchange house could mean the difference of a few hundred or even a few thousand dollars.

In addition, if you're concerned about which way a currency is moving versus the U.S. dollar, you can remove any future exchange risk by buying that currency ahead of time. Returning to our Italian farmhouse example, say you're planning to buy one next summer. Your budget is $200,000. You could exchange $200,000 now for euros, with the help of an exchange company, and then sit on those euros until time for closing. Again, this could work to your advantage or against you, but it could also allow you to sleep better at night between now and whenever you finally close on your euro purchase.

We've worked with a number of currency exchange companies over the years. Like banks, they merge and change name and new ones open up, so the best way to find one is simply to check online when you're ready to open an account. These companies are trading and moving currencies back and forth, one to another, all day every day and, therefore, can give you a better exchange rate than your bank. Opening an account with one is like opening a bank account, but you can do it all online. You'll have to provide basic know-your-client information. That accomplished, you have access to the group's better rates. This strategy can make particular sense if you know you'll be sending multiple wires for a renovation, staged preconstruction payments, or mortgage payments.

How and Why to Open a Local Bank Account Overseas

Sometimes you'll have the need to receive funds in another country directly. Maybe you'll want to wire your own funds from the United States to yourself in a place where you're renovating a house you've bought. If you invest in a rental, you'll need to be able to take receipt of the rent each month. In addition, as a property owner anywhere in the world, you'll have local expenses—property taxes, perhaps; other taxes; building fees; plus electric, gas, phone, cable, and Internet bills. We've known people who have tried to manage these things without benefit of a local bank account, but it's not easy and we'd say not worth it. The only reason to try to accomplish these things without a local bank account would be because you're unable to open a local bank account for some reason.

This isn't out of the question, because, unfortunately, it's not easy for an American to open a bank account in many parts of the world. It can be difficult, but it should almost never be impossible if you have a valid reason for wanting the account. Owning property in the country is a valid reason.

To open a bank account in another country, you'll need your passport, a second ID (your driver's license works), and a reference letter from at least one bank back home. You may also be asked for a reference letter from your attorney or your accountant. This is another reason to use a local attorney for your real estate transaction, because he or she will be able to provide a reference letter if you need one.

Be sure to ask about the bank's online access. You'll want to be able to check balances, move money, and, if possible, pay bills online. Most banks in most of the world offer online banking access. However, the level of service likely won't be what you are used to back home, and it may not be in English.

If you're investing in a rental property, we suggest opening a savings account as well as a checking account. This way, you can use the checking account as an operating account and move excess funds, as they accumulate, into the savings account. Don't keep a lot of money in your overseas checking account if you can help it. Forged checks and cloned automated teller machine (ATM) cards are not uncommon in some countries, and most banks in most of the world aren't going to make good if money is stolen from your account in either of these ways.

In that case, you may be wondering, wouldn't it be prudent to transfer excess funds, as they accumulate, from the foreign checking account to a U.S. savings or investment account? Typically, no. One big reason to be buying real estate overseas is for diversification, including currency diversification. If you transfer all the rental revenues that you earn from your rental property in another country to U.S. dollars in a U.S. bank account, you're interfering with your diversification agenda. One reason we bought an apartment in Medellín, for example, was to diversify into Colombia, the economy, and the currency.

When you accumulate funds enough in your overseas savings account to warrant it, you could consider other options for holding cash in that country. You could open a local certificate of deposit (CD), invest in the local stock market, use the money as the down payment on a next real estate purchase, or view the cash as a fund to cover personal expenses whenever you're in the country. Say you spend six months in France each year and rent your apartment out the rest of the year. You should (all things going according to plan and after all expenses and bills have been covered) end up with extra euros in your French bank account. You could use those euros to cover living expenses when you're in residence yourself, reducing your exchange rate risk. Rather than having to convert dollars to euros for every visit, you'll have cash earned as euros to spend as euros.

When You Exit

When you decide to sell, the proceeds from the sale can be deposited into your local bank account. Definitely, if the country where you're selling imposes currency restrictions, you'll want to have the funds put into your local account. Then you'll file the proper paperwork allowing you to wire the funds out of the country if that's your plan. Before returning that lump sum to U.S. dollars and to U.S. shores, consider your options. Remember that one big objective of the original property purchase was diversification. Bringing the proceeds from the sale of that piece of property back into the United States undermines that agenda.

If you're intending to buy something new in the same country, your decision is easy. Leave the money where it is until you're ready for your next purchase. If you're thinking of buying in another country, again, we'd suggest leaving the money where it is while you finalize your plans (unless the interim period extends indefinitely; in that case, you may want to find a better use for the sale proceeds in the meantime).

As an American, you'll have the same tax implications when you sell your overseas property as you would when selling a piece of property in the United States. If it's been your primary residence according to the IRS regulations, you can exempt gains from U.S. tax up to the current limits (right now that's $250,000 for a single taxpayer and $500,000 for a couple).

If you purchase rental property overseas, you'll then be required to file a Schedule E with your U.S. returns. You'll also be able to recognize associated depreciation of the asset for U.S. tax purposes (amortized over 40 years for foreign property). When you sell an overseas rental property, you'll be liable for depreciation recapture taxes along with any capital gain tax on the amount above your original basis.

You'll also likely have some tax obligation in the country where the property is located, although not all countries charge capital gains taxes on real estate (Croatia, New Zealand, and Argentina, for example, do not). Most countries that tax capital gains from the sale of real estate do so at particular rates separate from other income tax rates. A few countries tax gains on the sale of real estate as ordinary income, meaning the standard marginal tax bands determine the tax rate.

Don't worry about paying taxes twice on your gains. If your gain is taxable in both the country where the property is located and the United States, then you'll be able to take a tax credit on the U.S. side, limiting your total tax to the maximum due in either country. For example, if you pay 10% tax in the country where the property is located, then you'll pay another 5% or 10%, depending on your total income in the United States. If you pay 30% tax in the country where the property is located, then you'll owe nothing in the United States.

Note that, if the property is held by an entity, it is customary for the shares of the company to be sold (instead of the property itself), thus eliminating local transfer tax.

Can You Use the Proceeds in a 1031 Like-Kind Exchange?

One tax benefit available to U.S. investors in property overseas is the 1031 like-kind exchange. Briefly, this is a tax loophole that allows a real estate investor to defer tax on his gains by following specific rules allowing him to reinvest the proceeds from the sale of one property into the purchase of another. Most U.S. investors take advantage of this strategy when selling one piece of U.S. investment property to buy another.

This loophole works for U.S. taxpayers when they sell foreign property, as well, but only when the funds are invested in other foreign property. You can avoid tax on the gains by transferring the proceeds from one piece of property to the purchase of another, but it must be U.S. property for U.S. property or foreign for foreign.

Before using this tax rule with real estate overseas, be sure it makes sense. If you're paying a capital gains tax in the foreign country anyway, then the advantage of deferring your U.S. tax through a 1031 like-kind exchange probably isn't as great as taking the credit for the taxes paid in the other country. If you were, say, selling a piece of investment property in New Zealand, however, with the intention of using those proceeds to purchase another piece of investment property in Colombia, then the like-kind exchange could be a great benefit. You wouldn't be paying capital gains tax in New Zealand (as it doesn't charge any), so deferring U.S. tax is the right choice.

Appendix A
How to Do Overseas Cash-flow Math—www.liveandinvestoverseas.com/howtodooverseascashflowmath

We've created an interactive spreadsheet that should help you project monthly cash flow and net annual yield for any property you're considering buying overseas and to compare the return from renting the property short versus long term.

We've hosted the spreadsheet online so that you can play with variables to see the effect on your return on investment. You'll find it at www.liveandinvestoverseas.com/howtodooverseascashflowmath.

When you use the spreadsheet to help you think through a potential cash-flow investment, note the "Current Value" field. This allows you to estimate the current net yield over time, as the property value moves up or down. To start, your calculations will be based on the total purchase price of the property, including all closing costs.

Appendix B
Market Data

It's not easy to compile cost of buying and selling data. Search for it on the Internet, and you'll find conflicting facts and figures. This is because information like this can be unreliable on the Internet. It's also because these particulars change all the time. As well, currency exchange rates move in real time, meaning that today's costs in dollars can be irrelevant when you prepare to make a property purchase six months from today.

For each of the countries discussed in this book, therefore, we have compiled the following data with the help of on-the-ground contacts we trust:

- Restrictions on foreign ownership of land
- Real estate agent fees
- Attorney fees
- Notary fees
- Registration fees
- Transfer tax/Stamp duty
- Withholding tax
- Capital gains tax
- Rental income tax
- Property tax
- Bank financing terms (where relevant)
- Getting started resources

All this information is hosted on the following web page, which we update regularly: www.liveandinvestoverseas.com/realestatemarketdata.liveandinvestoverseas.com/realestatemarket data

Appendix C
Due Diligence Checklist

This list isn't comprehensive. Specific markets and types of properties require specific due diligence, but these are must-ask questions when buying anywhere in the world. Put them to both your attorney and your real estate agent and pay special attention when their responses differ (as they sometimes will).

What Is Your Budget?

We've discussed transfer taxes and other closing costs and the importance of including them when setting your budget for buying. Having $100,000 in your pocket doesn't mean you can buy a $100,000 property. Factor in all expenses and leave a little room in your budget for unforeseen costs that might come up.

What Comes with the Property?

Whether buying from a developer or a private seller, confirm what is included with the purchase. If you're investing in a short-term rental, maybe all furniture and appliances are included in the sale but maybe not. In many markets, it's common for the seller to take everything with him, down to the lighting fixtures. This can be a negotiating point when deciding how much to offer. Some developers in some markets don't include air conditioners, kitchen cabinetry, or even the kitchen sink and countertops when delivering new-built properties. In this case, adjust your budget to allow for the cost of their installation.

What Are the Zoning Rules?

If you're investing in a gated community, rules probably exist about what owners can and can't build. If you're buying in a mountain town in Ecuador, you could wake up one morning to find that the house next door has been converted to a disco. Should that happen, you'd have no recourse, as Ecuador doesn't impose zoning regulations. Find out before committing what your neighbors are prohibited from doing with their properties.

What Is Your Access?

This is a more critical question when buying in the countryside than in the city. The route a real estate agent follows when taking you to view a piece of land you're considering buying may or may not be the legal access to the property. You don't want to buy only to find out that the actual right of way is over two rivers and through the woods where there's no road.

Is There an HOA?

In the United States, we take for granted that any apartment building or housing development operates according to the rules of a Home Owners' Association (HOA). Don't assume this when buying an apartment or in a private community overseas, not even if the developer assures you that an HOA is in place. Ask to see the HOA documentation, including recent financial statements showing ongoing expenses and cash on hand, and have your attorney review it all, especially in Latin America. If the HOA isn't properly registered, the HOA rules, including those to do with the required payment of annual fees, are unenforceable. That can put your property value at risk.

How Much Is the HOA Fee?

You don't want to pay any more than you have to, but you also want to make sure the HOA fee is high enough to cover HOA expenses. If it isn't, property maintenance will be deferred, putting your investment at risk.

Are You Allowed to Rent Short Term?

Don't assume, even if you're buying from an investor who has been renting short term, that the property can legally be rented short term. Check relevant municipality legislation and the rules of the HOA. Short-term rentals can be restricted or disallowed by the local government or by building management.

How Far Away Are Day-to-Day Services?

As part of your property search process, take time to walk the neighborhood and explore the surrounding area to confirm services and amenities nearby. Where is the nearest grocery store, pharmacy, medical center, public transportation, bank, hardware store, and so forth? Depending on the market, these things can be as important to your occupancy rate as the property itself, especially when renting short term.

What Are the Total Carrying Costs?

Put pen to paper to calculate the total carrying costs, including property taxes, utility costs, Internet and cable, property management fees, and HOA expenses. You'll have these costs regardless of whether the property is rented. You should feel comfortable that you can cover them even without any rental income, and you should remember all of them when calculating your projected net rental yield.

If You're Buying a Second Home without Intending to Rent It, Who Will Watch the Property When You're Not There?

You'll probably need property-management services even if you don't plan to rent your property. You could engage a professional property manager to pay the bills, check on the property once in a while to make sure everything is okay, supervise cleaning (even if a property is unused, it should be cleaned regularly, especially in the tropics), and to oversee maintenance and repair work. Or you could enlist help from a neighbor-friend you trust, although this is probably more responsibility than most neighbors are up for.

Whatever strategy you employ, you need someone on the ground paying attention to your investment when you're elsewhere.

Does the Development Company Have a Track Record?

This is an especially important question when buying preconstruction. The greatest risk, even with an established developer, is that either the entire building or your particular unit won't be completed. More common is not completing construction on time. Research the developer's previous projects to see if he's met his promises in the past.

Appendix D
Understanding Your Tax Burden

Income Tax

Americans are taxed on their worldwide income no matter where in the world they're living. That means that, even if you move overseas to manage your cash-flow properties directly, you'll have to file a tax return with the IRS annually and you could owe them money. You may also have a tax filing and/or a tax payment requirement in the countries where you own properties. The possible permutations of what your tax situation might look like in the United States or in the countries where you might invest are many. You should seek professional tax advice, but here are some getting-started guidelines.

In the United States, you'll report rental income from properties overseas as you would report income from U.S. rental properties on Schedule E. You can take the same deductions for an overseas property as you would for one in the United States, with the exception of depreciation. It's calculated on a 40-year schedule for foreign properties.

If you invest in a farm property and aren't doing the farming yourself, the income should qualify as farm rental income category, which you report on Form 4835. Do the farm work yourself, and the income is reported on Schedule F. The important difference is that Schedule F income is charged as self-employment tax. Don't let your accountant tell you that you have to use Schedule F to report income from an agricultural investment when you're not doing the farm work yourself.

One benefit of buying investment property in places you like spending time is that you can deduct travel expenses when checking on your properties.

In the country where the property is located, your tax liability depends on whether you're living there. Spain, for example, charges 24% tax on gross rental income earned by a non-EU resident. Live in Spain or another EU (or EEA) country, and the tax is 19% of the net-rental-income earned (deductions aren't the same as you are allowed in the United States).

Other countries tax at source—that is, as the rental income is earned. Income from our rental property in Portugal was taxed at 25% after deducting the rental management fee. Our rental manager figured the tax and sent the amount owed to the Portuguese government. We got the balance. Because that was our only income in Portugal, no annual tax return was required.

Some countries treat rental income like regular income for foreigners. Because there's typically a minimum threshold before income tax is charged, you may not owe any tax on your rental income. In Panama, for example, the rate is 0% up to $11,000 of income. If your net rental income is less than $11,000, you owe no tax. However, you're still meant to file a tax return to report the income.

In a few cases, you may not owe any tax no matter how much revenue you've earned. Income from timber investments is tax exempt in many countries if the project is properly registered. Panama doesn't tax revenue from agriculture if the gross income for the farm is less than $350,000. Of course, an American is still liable for tax on that income in the United States.

For any tax you pay to another country for income that is also taxable in the United States, you can take a foreign tax credit on your U.S. tax return. Do this on Form 1116. Since depreciation of the property is allowed for U.S. taxes but is not allowed in many other countries, it's possible you could have less taxable income in the United States than you do in the other jurisdiction. Any foreign taxes that you can't take a credit for in one year can be carried forward to future years. If you do your own taxes on a program like TurboTax, the program can take care of the calculations and any carry-forward amounts.

Property Tax

Property taxes vary by country but typically amount to much less in most of the world than you're likely paying in the United States. In Belize, for example, your annual property tax on a $100,000 property might be $10. It will cost you more in gas to drive to the government office to pay the tax than the amount of the tax. Fortunately, Belize allows you to pay in advance. Keep your receipt in case the record of your payment is lost. It's Belize.

In many countries in Latin America, including Panama and Colombia, property taxes are paid quarterly. In Colombia, you'll receive your property tax bill in the mail. In Panama, you won't. You'll have to go (or send someone) to the property tax office to review the bill and pay it. Colombia has an online payment option. You'll need a local bank account to take advantage of it.

France imposes two taxes related to property—the *taxe foncière* and the *taxe d'habitation*. The first is the actual property tax. The second is an inhabitant tax. You'll pay both if you're renting your property short term. However, if you're renting long term, furnished or unfurnished, your tenant is meant to pay the *taxe d'habitation* if they're living in the apartment as of the first of January of that tax year.

Capital Gains Tax

Not all countries charge capital gains tax on real estate. Most that do impose a special rate, but a few tax capital gains as ordinary income.

New Zealand doesn't tax capital gains at all, not on real estate or on anything else. In France, you'll pay tax on capital gains from the sale of real estate according to a schedule that reduces the amount owed starting after five years of ownership. Hold the property for 22 years or more, and the capital gains tax is zero when you sell. Unfortunately, France has implemented an additional social tax on gains. This also is reduced over the time you own the property, starting with the sixth year, but it doesn't go away completely until you've owned the property for 30 years.

Some countries apply an inflation rate to adjust the gain calculation so it's based on a current value of the original purchase price. Some have exemption amounts that reduce the taxable gains.

Americans are liable for capital gains tax in the United States no matter where they live or where the property overseas is located. However, the foreign tax credit comes into play here, as well, and you shouldn't pay more in capital gains taxes than the highest applicable tax rate. For example, if you're taxed 10% on your gain in the foreign country and you fall into the 15% capital gains tax rate in the United States, you'd owe the IRS the 5% difference. Some deductions are allowed when calculating the gain.

Acknowledgments

Thank you to Werner and Bonnie for lending Lief the $5,000 that allowed him to make his first real estate investment in Chicago years ago.

Thank you to Bill and Mark, who introduced Kathleen to the idea of living and investing overseas in the first place.

Thank you to our attorney friends around the world, especially Morette Kinsella in Ireland, Juan Dario Gutierrez in Colombia, and Joao Figueira in Portugal, who have supported and protected our overseas real estate investing experiences over the decades.

And thank you to our *Live and Invest Overseas* readers. If not for you reading, what point to us writing.

Index